# a woman's guide to living alone

A Woman's Guide to

# living
# alone

## 10 Ways to Survive Grief and Be Happy

PAMELA STONE

TAYLOR TRADE PUBLISHING
*Lanham • Boulder • New York • Toronto • Plymouth, UK*

Copyright © 2001 by Pamela Stone

Published by Rowman & Littlefield
4501 Forbes Boulevard, Suite 200, Lanham, Maryland 20706
www.rowman.com

10 Thornbury Road, Plymouth PL6 7PP, United Kingdom

*Library of Congress Cataloging-in-Publication Data*
Stone, Pamela.
    A woman's guide to living alone : ten ways to survive grief and be happy / Pamela Stone.
        p.    cm.
    Includes bibliographical references and index.
    ISBN  978-0-87833-250-2
        1. Divorced women. 2. Widows. 3. Single women. 4. Middle age. I. Title.

HQ814 .S7937 2001
646.7'0086'52—dc21                                                 00-064885

Printed in the United States of America

# Contents

# Acknowledgments

This book could not have been created without the care and guidance of the following: My editors at the *Dallas Morning News*, namely Connie Dufner and Paula Watson, who allowed me to pursue dynamic stories on women's issues; Monday Night Writers' Group, who pored over my original material; Tejas Writers' Group, who advised me on the publishing process while never failing to boost my confidence; and to individual writers— Deborah Wormser, Neila Petrick, Dena Hill, and also Sally Ridgway Proler, my loving friend and mentor, one who has always cheered me on.

Special thanks goes to my agent, Jane Dystel, President of Jane Dystel Literary Management, who always believed in me and this project; she never lost sight of the importance of this book. To my editor, Camille Cline, whose gentle approach but firm hand helped shape this manuscript; and to the staff at Taylor Publishing, whose energy and dedication made this book come to life.

With great appreciation, I thank my husband, Jack Ciaccio, a great writer, who never lost sight of my goals. His patience and care helped me complete this effort.

In addition, I thank my brothers and sisters, who have always believed in me, and my parents, who are my angels looking on. My children, Jacque and Christin: thank you for enduring my chaotic spurts of creativity for your entire lives. Your spirit, strength, and sweetness have inspired me and nudged me on.

In closing, this book could not have been written without the powerful voices of the women interviewed. These women patiently shared their stories in hopes of touching others' lives. Without their honest testimonials, I would have no book. And readers would not have the opportunity to discover the joy of living alone.

# a woman's guide to living alone

## 10 Ways to Survive Grief and Be Happy

Meredith had the perfect marriage.

For 21 years, she and her husband rarely argued. They were close to their only child, and Meredith's husband, a wealthy Boca Raton entrepreneur, provided her with a lifestyle of golf, tennis, and trips to Europe.

Then, one day, her husband asked 47-year-old Meredith if he could have an affair with his secretary. Shocked, Meredith adamantly refused.

That night, he moved out and Meredith's world fell apart.

Like many women who become suddenly single, she wondered why her husband fell out of love with her.

She is not alone. According to experts, middle-aged women are the fastest-growing singles group. The National Center for Health Statistics reports that of women married before 1974, at least 50 percent have experienced divorce or widowhood. This figure is rapidly growing with the maturation of the baby boomers.

Losing husbands and lovers is never easy. Some women lose their men by choice; others have their loved ones stolen from them by illness and death. Their stories are painful and full of despair. But, after a time, these women turn a corner, and many discover the joy of living alone.

*A Woman's Guide to Living Alone: Ten Ways To Survive Grief and Be Happy* serves as a survival guide for these women. It focuses on women 35 and over who have experienced loss and overcome it. Many of these women found themselves suddenly alone. This book reveals what sustained them and what brought them through their grief.

Through interviews and testimonials, readers will meet numerous women who were painfully unaware of the demands of living alone. Whether through divorce or death of a spouse, these women had to adjust to their new independence. Many started new jobs. They established credit in their own names. And some raised their children by themselves.

They stumbled, struggled, and sometimes went hungry. But slowly, they began to rebuild their lives.

This is their story.

## Chapter One

# getting through the grief

When Susie Smoot-Brown returned to college after a divorce, she was raw from a marital breakup. She knew that anything was better than going home and crying night after night, so she did something about it.

While working in the college counseling office, she turned her grief into something positive. She started a support group for women going through the same experiences. "To me, divorce is like an amputation without a sedative, and all of us need to talk about it," she says.

Three years later, Ms. Smoot-Brown, now a college professor, continues to serve as the support group leader. She encourages women to share their feelings concerning their grief. Each week twelve women meet to discuss their progress as they try to rebuild their lives as singles. "I don't think you can drop a screen and say, 'That's the end of that feeling,'" Ms. Smoot-Brown tells her group of participants. "Progress is 'one step at a time,' a journey, and I see changes in this group each week."

Grief. It comes on like a heavy fog—filled with pain,

uncertainty, and fear. "Occasionally, the fog lifts," says Marilyn Dickson, a national grief consultant, "but you walk in it a long, long time."

**Barbara, 63.** Like many widows, her life came to a "screeching halt" the day her husband, Richard, died.

She discovered he had numerous personal debts. He was underinsured, and he had provided no college funds for their children. In addition to living alone, Barbara had to adjust to working full time as a receptionist in a friend's office. "Suddenly, I traded the status of being a dentist's wife for doing clerical work at little pay," says Barbara. "I was no longer accessible to my friends for lunch or club meetings. And I was taking orders from a person who I used to go to parties with. It caused me to lose my self-esteem—I was lonely and embarrassed by my situation."

A sense of alienation and depression is common among people who have lost a loved one. And, as in Barbara's case, it is not uncommon for people who suffer loss to experience feelings of panic and think: Will I ever get over this? Will my life be like before? Although you may not realize it, thousands of women discover the answer is usually *yes*.

## WHAT IS GRIEF?

Grief may occur in various stages: shock, denial, anger, depression, guilt, emotional release or letting go, and then acceptance. There may be physiological effects, too, including not sleeping, chest pains, rapid heartbeat, and so on. These feelings and manifestations may hit you like waves on a beach, coming and going at different times.

**DID YOU KNOW?**

- 32 percent of persons aged 65 and over live alone.
- There are over 13 million widowed people in the United States; over 11 million are women.
- There are 693,000 children under the age of 18 who live with a widowed parent.

s o u r c e : **U.S. Census Bureau, 1996**

- In 1995, 652,741 women were widowed in the United States.
- Of these, 35,821 were under the age of 44. Another 48,132 were between the ages of 45 and 54. 99,985 were between 55 and 64, 183,473 were between 65 and 74 years old, and 294,330 were older than 75 (these numbers are approximate).
- The average monthly Social Security benefit for a widow is $736.00.

s o u r c e s : **Vital Statistics Report, 1998 and Social Security Administration, 1998**

---

**Eleanor, 53.** Returning from a family reunion, Eleanor enjoyed driving the back roads of upstate New York. The air was crisp, and the leaves were turning from gold to rust. With the radio off, Eleanor felt calm for the first time in weeks.

Within an hour, though, the silence became too much, as a feeling of loneliness overwhelmed her. In spite of her professional accomplishments in the last year, Eleanor felt alienated. "I realized there was a good chance that I'd always be alone—that I'd never remarry," she says. "My divorce is the hardest lesson I've learned, and I'll always grieve over it. My fantasy was that I would have a healthy marriage, where my husband and I loved and respected each other. I'll never get over the fact that it didn't turn out the way I wanted it."

## WHAT ARE "SECONDARY LOSSES"?

Has your husband died or left? Was he the breadwinner, the money manager, or the handyman? If you assumed only the role of homemaker, then you may face definite changes in your lifestyle.

When a spouse dies or leaves, the skills that disappear with them are "secondary losses." You must learn them yourself, which can be overwhelming.

SOURCE: **AARP**

## HOW LONG DO WE GRIEVE?

For an average person (which nobody really is), the grieving period is from 18 months to three years. The stages of grief do not come in neat little boxes. They may come all at once or off and on throughout the years, and in no particular order.

Referring to grief in stages is sometimes misleading," says Richard Gilbert, author of *Responding to Grief* (Spirit of

Health, 1999), "because it implies that we get done with it. *Grief is about surviving.* We get through the pain, but from time to time, we will always grieve."

"Whatever the loss," adds Rev. Gilbert, "we're not going to stop remembering our loved ones. After seven years, some memories are still fresh. And they will be with us forever."

## GETTING THROUGH THE GRIEF

Many women believe that to "endure and hang on" is all you have to do to get through your grief. Grief experts disagree. "When we participate actively, we come out stronger and more whole," says Marilyn Dickson, who is affiliated with the Association of Death and Educational Counseling in Muncton, New Hampshire. Similarly to training for a race, grief forces us to use our natural, human resources—talking, weeping, and writing.

"When a person is widowed or divorced," says Ms. Dickson, "their identity is threatened, and they ask 'who am I?'"

You've always lived as a couple, and suddenly you aren't a couple. Being single is a shock. Being without a partner shakes you to your very bones. It makes you feel vulnerable and alone.

But these feelings are temporary. They're part of growing and learning to live alone. And learning to like yourself in the process.

Ms. Dickson conducts numerous grief groups throughout the year, giving women the opportunity to meet other women who share the same experiences. "Sometimes strangers can be more beneficial to those in grief because they are more honest and open," she says. "Old friends tend to tell you what you want to hear. Strangers don't have to guard their words."

Did you also know that strangers can make the best of friends? Sometimes, people you meet in support groups or in singles' groups can form strong relationships, because you don't have any history with them. They also don't bring unnecessary baggage to the friendship. Because of this, they may be more objective and open in their opinions.

**Susie Smoot-Brown, college professor.** Ms. Smoot-Brown says that many women facing loss walk the same path. At her college, newly single women are returning to further their education. "They are anxious about how they will juggle work, family and school. They are unsure of their academic capabilities, and they feel isolated and alone."

Through her support group, she allows these women to express their grief and anxieties, while giving them the opportunity to develop a new circle of friends.

## SIGNS OF GRIEF

**Adrian, 38.** Five months after Adrian lost her husband, she threw herself into her work as an insurance adjuster. Business meetings, sales calls, writing memos, and making presentations filled her days. The long hours kept her from thinking, feeling. One day, she entered the elevator at her office and caught a whiff of her husband's cologne on another man. This triggered the memory of her husband dressed for work, brushing past her in the

## WHAT YOU CAN DO WHEN A LOVED ONE MOVES ON

1. Encourage your family to acknowledge the loss.
2. Listen to yourself, and take yourself seriously in a gentle, healthy way.
3. Respect how family members may each react differently to the loss. The needs of one could be different from the needs of another.
4. Talk about your feelings and share the memories.
5. Find new rituals to share with loved ones.
6. Work through feelings of grief to bring closure to the pain and loss.

kitchen. On his way out the door, she remembers him tenderly kissing her on the cheek.

Standing in the middle of the elevator, clutching her briefcase, Adrian smiled. The memory was crystal clear. Then, her eyes filled with tears. When she reached her floor, she was unable to move, she was crying so hard.

Memories, senses, feelings. They well up in us after a loss. Whether from divorce or death, these memories are part of us. They are real and powerful. And they should not be ignored.

These feelings may strike us at inconvenient times, but they are a natural part of grieving. If we try to hide these feelings, they could come to haunt us at other times in our lives, causing serious repercussions.

Feeling our feelings is a part of the grieving process,

and it's healthy for us to express them, says Rev. Richard Gilbert, a grief consultant. He suggests that those of us who are dealing with loss should acknowledge the loss. "The pain of grief and the traumas of the world can leave us feeling lost, alone, and abandoned," he concludes. "But through our spiritual connections we learn to trust again."

### GRIEVING AFTER A DIVORCE

The grief that follows a divorce is often tumultuous. "It's like a terrible thunderstorm that runs its course," says Dr. Arthur Kovacs, a Santa Monica psychologist. He describes a person going through divorce as one who expresses emotions by weeping uncontrollably, temper tantrums, even threats of suicide. Unfortunately, it's not uncommon for children to witness this behavior. During this time, one may also feel alone and isolated. But there is hope.

SUGGESTIONS: Don't isolate yourself from others, says Dr. Kovacs. Don't allow yourself to shut down emotionally. Look to friends or family for nurturing and support.

## HOLIDAYS ARE DIFFICULT

When we are grieving, we are frequently blind-sided. Our senses are heightened. We get reminders we don't expect—a whiff of someone's perfume or smoke from a pipe. The touch of silk or soft jersey can remind us of a person, and the sight of a scarf or jacket can cause familiar scenes to flash before our eyes.

These memories are meaningful and precious, yet they may come at embarrassing times. Still, there is no way to control them.

There's no time limit on these memories, either. That's why holidays are so hard on people who've lost someone. Holidays are public occasions where others are doing things together that you and your husband used to do. And now you can't.

So when facing the holidays, it's important to be prepared. Recognize that you will be dealing with the days and times that remind you of your deceased or divorced spouse. You will be dealing with the memories of his illness or death, or his separation from you, and it's important to realize that these times will be difficult for you.

As holidays approach, ask yourself: Which family traditions are important? Which ones should you continue? Which ones should you change?

Perhaps your grown children could have the holiday dinner at their house. "Remember, there will be an *empty chair* at your holiday dinner. You must prepare for it," says Ms. Dickson.

And what about gift-giving?

If your spouse is deceased and the thought of exchanging gifts without him being there is too painful, you might consider alternatives like these: Perhaps you could ask family members to contribute to the American Heart Association or the Cancer Society or another non-profit organization in your husband's name. Or each person could buy an ornament for your Christmas tree and put their name on it with a message to their dad.

After a loss, if you don't plan for the holiday, making concessions to the fact of the loss, it's harder. People enduring a loss should change customs and create new family rituals.

As we grieve, a reorganization takes place. People reinvest themselves emotionally and psychologically in the future. And keeping grief under a tight lid may cause multiple problems.

## WHO HAS TIME TO GRIEVE?

Some women feel they do not have time to grieve. They are consumed with surviving, and they do not have time to reflect on the past.

**Karen, 43.** As she and her husband awaited the birth of their third child, due in a few weeks, they couldn't have been happier. It was Christmas. The lights were strung, the tree decorated, and the dining room table filled with wrapping paper and velvet ribbon, awaiting the new gifts.

As Karen's husband, Peter, prepared to take their 15-year-old daughter shopping, he suddenly had a sharp pain in his stomach. Within seconds, he crumbled onto the floor writhing in pain. "Take me to the hospital immediately!" he cried out.

His family quickly whisked him to the hospital, where he was diagnosed with an acute case of pancreatitis.

When Karen returned to the hospital early the next morning, she was shocked to find they were preparing her husband for emergency surgery. In a daze, she signed the papers and kissed her husband goodbye. "That was the last time he spoke to me," she says sadly.

After spending almost three weeks in the ICU, Peter's condition worsened. His pancreas malfunctioned, spilling poisonous enzymes throughout his body. The doctors finally came to Karen, saying, "He's not going to make it." They suggested the family take him off life support.

Karen remembers standing by her husband's side. She and her daughters kissed him goodbye and then waited in horror and disbelief. "I watched the heart monitor until it wouldn't go anymore," she says, her eyes filling with tears.

But that was just the beginning of her trials. Two days later Karen experienced lower-back pain at her husband's funeral service. Although she tried to ignore it, she knew it was labor. After the funeral guests left her home, she began to clean. In a fury, she washed the dirty dishes, mopped the floors, did three loads of laundry, ironed, and vacuumed. At 5 A.M. the next morning, she called her son-in-law and asked him to take her to the hospital.

An eight-and-half-pound boy was born at midday. She named him Peter, after his father. As the hospital visitors filled the room, Karen looked like a Swedish beauty. Her long blonde hair was braided. As she proudly showed off her infant, you'd never have guessed that she'd buried her husband the day before.

Grief? Karen didn't have time for that. Like many

women after a sudden death, she was consumed with attending to her physical and financial needs.

On the way home from the hospital, she dropped by to show her new infant boy to her husband's parents. After admiring the baby, her father-in-law took her aside, saying, "Don't think you can call on us to help you financially, because we can't. We just don't have the means."

Karen was shocked. She thought her in-laws would do anything to help their grandson. But she was wrong. "Faced with that thought, I came home and prepared to do whatever I needed to for myself and my family. There wasn't any other choice."

In an instant, Karen not only lost her life partner, but also her business partner. Peter had been an architect and builder and Karen had kept his books and tended to other details of his business and finances. However, she was not able to go out and get new clients like Peter could.

With little insurance and few benefits, Karen acted quickly. She turned her part-time catering business into a full-time endeavor. She also rented her luxury home to a rock star for a three-month period. Then she moved into a rented house with her children. Within a few months' time, Karen had experienced a death, a birth, a location move, and the startup of a new business.

"During the first year, I tended to my physical needs," she explained. "I did charity ball catering, and I didn't mind asking for the business of friends I'd formerly socialized with. I had no problem with that.

"Maybe I was desperate, but I didn't let my pride stand in the way of the needs of my family. I didn't want to lower my standard of living. I wanted to keep it steady for my children."

At what point was Karen able to grieve?

"Peter was on my mind constantly," she said. After attending a grief-counseling group at church and a memorial service for her husband, she had little time to continue grieving. Often, though, she would become consumed with anger. "I'd wonder why he would've left me with all this. In fact, I still do."

### WHAT ABOUT ME?

Are you spending all your time comforting others? Remember to take care of yourself during the grieving process. Join a support group. Allow yourself tears and feelings. As we cry, so do our children, and this is healthy. By showing them your pain, you allow them to express their pain. Be good to yourself. Pamper yourself.

### DAY-TO-DAY LOSS

Many women flinch at the word "widow." They associate it with a loss that continues through time, permanently. Yet we're conditioned to believe *you must have a partner in life. Always.*

**Liz Carpenter, veteran Washington insider.** When Ms. Carpenter, one of journalism's truly trend-setting heroines, lost her husband, she was just 52 and felt lost. In her book, *Getting Better All The Time* (Simon and Schuster, 1987), she describes it this way: "We had tasted the excitement and champagne of life together, shared the successes and disappointments of pursuing careers together, and raised a family together. Now, when I was only 52, my husband was dead. And the champagne was flat."

"We didn't know what happiness was," she reflects. "That was us—living so fast that we didn't stop and say, 'Hey, hold everything, this is happiness.'"

## HOW GRIEF AFFECTS FAMILY MEMBERS

When someone departs our life, it's like ripples moving across a lake. Eventually, the loss reaches out beyond the spouse to touch others as well. Sons, daughters, brothers, sisters, uncles, aunts, cousins, and friends are affected. And whether your children are small or grown, their grief is just as painful.

When you are involved in your own grief, how do you attend to others? Simply being there for them is a big help. Then, *just let them express their grief freely*. All family members need time to heal.

## FAMILY CELEBRATIONS

After Nell's husband John died, she called together her children and her sister's family to "celebrate" her husband's death. A nature lover, her husband felt more at home outdoors at his lake house than in his office. He was an avid fisherman. And he loved bird watching and working in his garden. He also loved his privacy.

When he became terminally ill with cancer, John decided to spend his last days at home, not in the hospital. With the help of hospice care, he lay comfortably in bed while family and friends came to visit. They played the guitar, told jokes, and exchanged hilarious family stories. Instead of dying in the hushed, sterile silence of a hospital, John's last days were filled with warmth, laughter, and love, creating precious memories for those left behind.

At the end, the family planted a peach tree and buried John's ashes beneath it. It was their way of paying tribute to his life past, and wishing him well in the life to come.

### THE WHOLE FAMILY IS CHANGING

Unfortunately, grief is not confined to one person alone. Although you may not be aware of it, your entire family is grieving for the loss of your spouse. After a loss, all family members are forced to find new roles for themselves. They are wondering who will take over the lost person's duties and responsibilities. As this readjustment occurs, family members are forced to change and assume new roles. How will they react to this replacement?

## SHOULD CHILDREN ATTEND FUNERALS?

If children are not frightened by the funeral process, attending the funeral with their parents may make them feel included in the celebration of the deceased's life. Just standing side by side with their loved ones in tribute to the dead may be comforting to children.

At an Italian funeral in New Orleans, a woman's eldest daughter, 8, was allowed to write a note and place it in her father's coffin. Today, that same note is also inscribed on the father's tomb. It reads:

"You are always in our heart, our memories will never part."

The specific circumstances surrounding the loss of a husband and father will certainly affect how the various family members react afterward. Consider the following situation.

A successful businessman and loving father traveled to a nearby college town to visit his daughter. After taking her to dinner, celebrating her good grades and progress in school, he returned to his hotel. There, he signed ten suicide notes and injected himself with an overdose of drugs.

The four children were devastated. Encouraging her children to find closure for their own pain, as well as to try to forgive their father, Connie, the mother, encouraged them to leave notes in his coffin. This became their way of saying goodbye.

Now when the family gathers at Christmas, the children, ages 9 to 24, write individual notes to their father. Some tell him how well they're doing in school. Others express their hopes, their fears, and their anger. A few wish him well. As they seal their notes and carefully place them under the tree, Connie sighs with relief. "At least they're trying," she says. "As they communicate their feelings to their father, this helps them come to terms with his suicide."

However, in this traumatic case, the four children were still reeling from shock two years later. One daughter became bulimic and was caught shoplifting laxatives on her college campus. One son is almost suicidal and is withdrawn from the family. And the youngest child still struggles with "why her daddy left her."

Connie, 46, has gone from anger to depression to dogged determination. She fights for survival daily—for herself and for her children.

In order to care for her own emotional needs, she joined a support group for families of suicide victims, and she has received financial help from her church and her daughter's school, which has waived tuition. And in the middle of fighting daily battles, Connie has not lost touch with the grief of her children.

Whether lighting a candle, planting a tree, writing a note to their father, or singing a song, paying tribute to a person's memory becomes a meaningful ritual.

## TIME TO GRIEVE

In our culture, we rush through the funeral service, briefly meet with relatives, and are expected to return to work or a regular routine in a few days or less. This is extremely difficult and unrealistic. Experts warn of the danger in not taking the time to grieve. They suggest avoiding a set agenda or rituals dictated by others.

If your faith doesn't have a built-in grieving time, create your own. Take time off from work, slow down, and allow yourself to grieve by remembering your loved ones. You may want to visit a park. Drive to a mountain top. View the sunset from a spot that was appreciated by your spouse. Or you may want to just sit and relax in your husband's study, surrounded by the books, paintings, and other items he loved. It's okay to close your eyes and feel his presence. It's okay to talk to your husband. It's okay to say goodbye your own way, in your own time.

There's more to grief than just mourning the loss of a loved one. Grief also involves the loss of a dream, a lifestyle, or something that's always been permanent in our lives, like our childhood home. Enduring a loss affects not only you, but your children and your children's children. The dynamics are changed. Places are changed. Values and expectations are changed. Your family, friends, and neighbors are all forced to readjust.

## DEALING WITH GRIEF IN OLDER CHILDREN

When Ella, 72, sold her home and asked her son to pack up her husband's treasures, she had no idea it would be so emotional for him. After all, her son, Jeffrey, was 42 years old.

Packing up his dad's things from the study—his books, magazines, pipe, and memoirs from World War II— brought tears to Jeffrey's eyes. He gently wrapped each item and placed it in a box, where they would remain, like a childhood memory.

Packing up his dad's personal items and closing the family home was more painful than he anticipated, says Jeffrey.

He knew that his mother, a widow, needed to move into an assisted-living center for medical reasons. Still, he couldn't ignore the fact that shutting down his childhood home was difficult. "With every box I packed and every bag I dragged to the garbage, I felt lost, like I was losing something," he said.

He is not alone. Many aging baby boomers struggle as their parents "move on," whether to active retirement lifestyles or to nursing homes. Either way, adult children often feel left behind.

Ken, 54, a pastoral care counselor, experienced feelings of confusion when his mother sold the farm in Wauseon, Ohio, where she and his dad had lived for 30 years.

"I can remember when my mother moved into town in 1989. All of a sudden, I felt lost," he said. "It seemed strange not going back to the farm. I liked the house she moved to—it was pleasant, and my mother was happy. But I had mixed feelings. In the past, it was okay if I moved, but I never had to deal with my parents moving."

Irene Goldenberg, family psychologist at the Los Angeles Psychiatric Center, University of California, believes "feeling uprooted" by parents moving on is common. When a change takes place in a family, like a death or divorce, she explains, the whole system reacts. It changes everybody's role. "Traditions and places represent a sense of identity and security. They give you a sense of being part of something other than yourself," she says. "People's roots are attached to the home where they grew up. Age doesn't matter. In our hurried world today, with all its pressures, children like depending on the older generation to remain unchanged."

Samuel Romano, a clinical psychologist at the Department of Family Practice, University of Michigan Medical School in Chelsea, feels that many people grieve when their parents "move on."

"When the household is disrupted, we hold onto things," he says. Objects and places symbolize experiences or give meaning to our lives. Like looking through old photos with loved ones, the sharing of the ritual is important. "Show the symbols and share them with others," he advises.

But realize that these feelings of pain are a transitory thing, he adds. "This is another developmental shift. It is important to understand the loss, accept it, mourn it, and move forward."

## THE VALUE OF SUPPORT GROUPS

Thelma's entire life revolved around her husband. Even though she held a full-time job, her husband provided her with a life of security, love, and laughter. After all, he was her best friend. After his sudden death, she found herself lonely and bitter. "I valued our marriage. We worked hard at it, and now I was suffering because a light had gone out of my life."

Upon request from a friend, she reluctantly joined a support group. There, she met other women going through the same emotions. "Being listened to in the group gave me hope. It took away my hurt. Gradually, I realized there may be a future for me."

"I have four families now," says Thelma proudly. "They are my biological family, my friends from work, my church, and my support group."

## CHAPTER 1 REVIEW: GETTING THROUGH THE GRIEF IS YOUR FIRST STEP TO SURVIVING HAPPILY

- **What is grief?** It hovers like a dark cloud, filling you with pain, uncertainty, and fear. It appears as shock, denial, guilt, anger, depression, longing, letting go, and at last, acceptance.
- **How long do we grieve?** While each of us is different, a rule of thumb is that the main grieving period may last from 18 months to 3 years.
- **Allow yourself time to grieve.** Don't rush the process. If it's a divorce, you are also grieving for the loss of your family as it was.
- **Signs of grief.** Memories, sense, and feelings well up in us after a loss. They are a natural part of grieving, and they should be recognized.
- **Why holidays are difficult.** In a word, "tradition." That's why it's important to consider which traditions to continue and which ones you may want to change or put aside. You should feel free to change customs and create new family rituals.
- **It's not only your grief.** Loss affects the entire family: parents and grandparents, uncles, aunts, brothers, sisters. Family members of all ages are touched by grief, and they need time to deal with it, so healing can take place.
- **Encourage children to attend the funeral.** If children are not frightened by the funeral process, being part of it and feeling included in the ceremony for the deceased may help them emotionally.

- **Give yourself time to grieve.** If your faith doesn't have a built-in grieving time, create your own. Take time off from work and routines. Slow down and allow yourself to grieve by remembering your loved ones.
- **Pay tribute to the deceased.** Create an altar, visit a mountaintop, browse through the deceased's favorite books, sew a quilt for him, or write in a journal. Think about this person and all he means to you.
- **Helping older children to accept the loss.** You've decided to pack up your husband's belongings and move to Florida. Why may this move be so difficult for your grown children? Even as adults, the emotional pull of one's memory can sometimes be overwhelming. Older children feel displaced when there's a loss in the family. As you pack up your spouse's belongings, share some memories with your family. This will help them accept the loss.

## Chapter Two

# learning to let go

Emily, 50, stared long and hard into the fire. Her face was calm, her movements deliberate.

Slowly, she sorted through a box of family pictures, selecting snapshots of herself and her ex-husband, Jeffrey. As she gently touched each photo, the memories came flooding back. Birthdays, anniversaries, holidays, and weddings. Twenty-eight years of married life. Poignant memories. Happy memories. Painful memories. And most recently, memories of divorce, which she'd like to forget. Each photo was significant. Emily was determined to make a ritual out of these memories. She decided to hold a cremation. One by one, she gently kissed each picture, blessed it, and threw it into the fire.

As she watched the crimson flames, she says, she "realized the fire symbolized the richness and beauty of our relationship. It was my way of letting go."

Letting go. Some women fight loss with rage. They rant and rave and throw their husband's clothes out on the lawn, puncture his tires, or, like Bernadine in the movie *Waiting to Exhale,* stuff their husband's designer suits into his shiny BMW and set it on fire.

## CELEBRATING RITUALS

But Emily, a therapist, took another approach. She "celebrated" the separation of her husband from her life with a cremation. "We are not a ritualistic society," she says. "When you give up a behavior, it's important to memorialize it by doing something physical. I needed to do *something* to symbolize the break in my marriage."

As Emily watched the flames burning the photos into ashes, she was fascinated by the steps of the cremation process. "I don't think of it as *getting rid of,*" she admits. "It was more like getting *through.*"

Performing rituals is a tool for letting go of emotional ties. But in the case of family celebrations, this can also pose problems.

For Emily, becoming emotionally distant from her ex was difficult, especially since they were grandparents and were often invited to the same family gatherings. When her grandson was born, she and her husband had been separated only a month. "Here was this great blessing and joy that I was excited about. And at the same time, there was enormous pain in not sharing it with Jeffrey. It was really hard."

When Emily speaks of Jeffrey, her pale blue eyes turn the color of slate. At first, she speaks haltingly, searching for the right words, then her soft voice becomes harsh.

"I was devastated by this divorce. It was not my

choice. He'd had an affair at 40, but it was over. After his 50th birthday, though, he became obsessed with aging and dying."

A few months later, he attended a spiritual retreat. When he returned home, her husband admitted to having met someone. "The next day he moved out," says Emily flatly.

Emily and Jeffrey, high school sweethearts, were married when they were both 20. "More of my life was spent with him than without him," she says. "We grew up together. We parented each other. So much of myself was enmeshed in him."

Three years after the divorce, Emily was amazed to find that her pain was still intense at times. While attending a family backyard party, she saw Jeffrey's new wife. "I couldn't bring myself to shake her hand. I stood in the midst of the group and let my feelings burn."

"I wasn't trying to be my nice usual self," she says. "Basically, I was dying to scratch her eyes out. I felt rage and jealousy—Jeffrey seemed so glib and happy, and he was getting on with his life."

Although Emily realized that "feeling the rage" was healthy, she needed an outlet for her anger. Today, she's part of a writing group, where she's working on a short story about a woman who murders her ex. Emily smiles devilishly, saying, "It's a suspense tale with a delicious plot."

As more and more women experience divorce, they often find themselves in turmoil. Some have been married to the same person for more than half their lives. Some grew up together, sharing a history with their ex. Even if they welcome the separation or divorce, that person continues to push their emotional buttons.

**Meredith, married 21 years.** When she was faced with divorcing her husband after 21 years of marriage, Meredith found it difficult to let go. For two years, her husband stalled the divorce proceedings. The couple fought bitterly. Finally, in desperation, Meredith walked away. "I had to get on with my life, and in order to do so, I gave him everything," she says. "My daughter and I left our home with nothing but the shirts on our backs. I left my mother's china, my automobile, and most of my possessions. I knew the only way for me to emotionally leave my husband was to walk away from our divorce."

It has been more than six years since her divorce. Meredith looks back on those years as the hardest in her life.

Immediately after her divorce, she pushed herself into a job as a realtor, working seven days a week. At the time, she says, her daughter was in prep school, and she was living alone for the first time in her life.

Today, Meredith is a top producer in her field and she enjoys being single in Boca Raton, Florida, where she continues to share friendships with old and new acquaintances. "After my divorce, I had no idea that I could do it on my own. But I knew I was going to survive, because I am too proud, and I would never allow myself to fail."

## STOP BETTING ON A DEAD RELATIONSHIP

In his book *Rebuilding: When Your Relationship Ends* (Impact Publishers, 1992), Dr. Bruce Fisher says: "Disentangling is hard to do—it's tough to let go of the strong emotional ties which remain from a dissolved love union." Nevertheless, he adds, "It is important to stop investing emotionally in a dead relationship."

One way is to find positive outlets for your emotions. In Meredith's case, her work helped her "disentangle" as she discovered her capabilities as a provider.

**Verdell Davis, widow.** Ms. Davis is another example of a person who struggled with letting go. Married at 18 to a dynamic Southern Baptist minister, she'd spent most of her life living happily in his shadow.

In 1987, after her husband's death in an airplane crash, she was thrown into intense grieving and depression.

In her book *Let Me Grieve, But Not Forever* (Word, 1997), Ms. Davis describes her experiences in letting go.

> In major losses, our identity, our security, our perceptions, our dreams, our relationships—indeed, the whole of our lives change, and we must let go of what we cannot keep. We must turn loose of the past and the things that tend to hold us captive, even after they are long gone. . . . Letting go of Creath [her husband] was very hard, and it took a very long time. I needed him for my life to make sense, at least I needed the memory of him. I needed an identity, if not as his wife, then as his widow, and I was learning to walk with half of me gone. . . . I needed to talk about him until the richness we had together mellowed into my inner being and no longer needed expression to be real. I needed to hold on to him while I wrestled with the issues of faith, and

trust, and who God is in the darkness. . . . I needed to
be Mrs. Creath Davis until I could sign my name
Verdell Davis without having to think about it.
. . . Somewhere along the way, letting go became a
choice I had to make.

Ms. Davis is now a writer and grief consultant. As she
learned to let go of her husband "one step at a time," she
realized she couldn't live the rest of her life clinging to
what was familiar and secure. After her husband died, she
became the newly appointed director of her school, where
she'd worked as an administrator for several years. All at
once, she was faced with increasing demands, as well as
grieving for her husband.

Inside her, says Ms. Davis, there was a voice pleading,
"Your world is changing. Your life is changing. It's okay to
'go with it' and pursue your dream as a writer."

"So, contrary to the safe, secure Verdell of the past, the
woman who craved security as a blanket, I chose adventure," says Ms. Davis. She quit her job. And wrote a book
based on her grieving.

"I let go of the trapeze I was holding without seeing
another one clearly in sight," laughs Verdell. "And I'm not
sure how I did it."

## STOP DESTRUCTIVE BEHAVIOR PATTERNS

Marriage and family counselor Bruce Drobeck says
that disentangling from one's spouse is often difficult, because a legal divorce does not necessarily mean the individuals have emotionally separated.

"After divorce, a power struggle still exists with most couples, and the children are often caught in the middle," Dr. Drobeck says. "Often there is a tug-of-war between couples, where they continue to push each other's emotional buttons. Some couples continue destructive behavior patterns which began early in the marriage."

To break this pattern, Dr. Drobeck suggests allowing for a natural grieving process—"experiencing the feelings of denial, anger, loss, pain, guilt, and later, acceptance."

He suggests not dwelling too long on any stage of recovery. "If you spend an inordinate amount of time thinking about your ex or being angry, this will prevent you from getting on with your life."

**Sherry, married over 20 years.** When Sherry speaks of the decline of her marriage, she remembers it all. Every date. Every known affair. The emotional abuse. The broken promises. The broken dreams. Although she doesn't regret the breakup, she does regret the effect it had on her children. She regrets breaking up their home, but, under the circumstances, it was the only way.

When her husband moved out, she went to bed and cried for days. "I wasn't crying for him, but for the loss of my marriage. The loss of a family."

In desperation, she began writing her husband a letter. "I told him all the things I'd failed to express in our marriage." Although she never gave her husband the letter, it started her writing in a journal.

## JOURNALING IS AN OUTLET

Journaling became an outlet for Sherry's grief. "I kept writing and writing, saying all the things I'd failed to say before. Anger, hurt, pain—it all poured out. I'd never admitted to anyone about our poor marriage, I was so ashamed. But when writing, I couldn't stop myself.

"The more I wrote, the better I felt."

After the divorce, she took two jobs to support her family. In spite of her busy schedule, she read every self-help book on divorce she could find. "Then, from my readings, I began to write notes of encouragement to myself in a notebook which I carried in my purse."

"I was so vulnerable at that time. I was desperate for help," she says. Through reading and writing, Sherry's anger slowly dissipated. In the end, she describes her recovery this way: "It's such a long journey to find yourself and to realize that you're going to be okay."

While it is difficult to emotionally separate from a spouse after a divorce, it is sometimes harder after a loved one has died.

## BREAKING TIES AFTER A DEATH

Married for the first time at the age of 41, Louise's husband, John, died barely five years later.

Petite, with soft, curly hair, Louise has a dimpled smile. She speaks in a strong, clear voice. Dressed in a cotton over-blouse and shorts, she sits on the edge of her sofa, and seems eager to share her story. She pulls no punches.

"I miss him. He was the love of my life," says Louise, speaking of her husband, her eyes filling with tears.

"I miss his laughter and his wisdom. Making decisions is now difficult . . .

"I remember sitting in the same room with John while I told him about a frustrating teaching day. He'd be typing a report and smoking his pipe, but I knew he was listening," says Louise.

Louise, an elementary school teacher, lost her husband a few weeks after a failed bypass surgery. Her anger was bitter. "I had unhealthy relationships, until I met John. Now, he's gone. I loved him deeply . . . and I was furious about being alone again."

Like Sherry, Louise began writing in a journal. Without thinking, she began writing to an imaginative character called "Alone," whom she often angrily cursed. "From complaining about a difficult child at school to recalling my husband's death, I got it all out," she said. "I realized I needed to get the negative out before I could start writing positively."

Then, Louise went one step further. She read parts of her journal to her grief group. "Being able to share these emotions helped tremendously. I realized a lot of these feelings were normal," she says. "In my grief group, I learned to talk about how I felt. I felt like I'd been knocked into the Grand Canyon and barely survived.

"I felt valueless."

As she revealed her inner feelings to the group, she began to grow. "When you share gut-level feelings, you get close fast," Louise says. That summer, her emotions became more positive when she commemorated her husband's death by visiting a place he loved: Pikes Peak near Colorado Springs, Colorado.

While feeding the chipmunks on top of Pikes Peak, she felt her husband's presence. She recalled how the mountains were sacred and meaningful to John, and it was a healing experience.

Although she found an outlet for her roller-coaster emotions, Louise still must cope with being alone. But memories of her husband help her get through difficult days. She remembers his touch, his gentleness, his beautiful singing voice, and his sharp wit. "I miss his laughter. I miss his wisdom. I miss hearing him softly snore beside me at night. But I'm happy for our time together. And as long as I live, I'll always remember seeing the love in his eyes when I walked into a room."

It has been four years since her husband died, and Louise is getting on with her life. On her 50th birthday, she asked friends from near and far to join in her celebration. While seated in a circle, the group toasted their friendship with vintage champagne. "At this point, I knew I was on my way to healing—at last, I was getting through my grief."

Whether you are breaking emotional ties after death, divorce, or separation, it is vital that you acknowledge your grief. Before you learn to let your grief go, you must express it and react to it. This process takes time. Through counseling, prayer, rituals, and support from friends or grief groups, hopefully you will learn to grieve . . . and to remember.

You may value the good memories, and learn to forgive the bad ones, recalling your shared history with this person. With time, if you work hard on these steps, you can discover a new freedom and vitality. You will discover the ability to let go . . . and learn to love yourself in the process.

## LETTING GO OF OUR CHILDREN

But what happens when letting go affects our children?

**Penelope's situation.** When Penelope dropped her child off at daycare, he cried hard, bellowing like a small cow. Hurriedly, she kissed him goodbye and handed him to the child care worker. As she drove off, she could see him tearfully waving at her.

This was too much, thought Penelope. Newly divorced, she hated leaving her toddler with strangers. Before her breakup, she worked flex-time, which allowed her to remain at home with her child. She felt unsettled about this daycare decision. She'd never planned it this way.

Although the daycare worker assured her that it was natural for her 18-month-old child to feel anxious, Penelope still felt guilty. Sensing her apprehension, her child cried more and more each day.

What should she do?

Clinical psychologist Dr. Mary Ann Little believes that parents experience separation anxiety throughout a child's lifetime. And separation due to death or divorce, although painful, is yet another transition.

Separation anxiety occurs the first time a parent allows a child to walk alone, to jump from a diving board alone, or to solve a conflict with friends without interference, she says.

Dr. Little, author of *Loving Your Children Better* (Westport, 1991), says learning to let go means letting go of expectations and attachments. It occurs when children enter preschool for the first time, when they go on their first sleep-over, when they go off to summer camp, or when they go off to college.

"I feel those transitions should be built upon gradually," Dr. Little says. "And, step by step, children learn to succeed independently."

"When a family is experiencing a loss, the parent is struggling with some guilt, wondering if she should leave the child or how it will affect the child's development," says Roberta Bergman, senior vice president of The Child Care Group, a non-profit United Way Affiliate which provides child care management services for the United States Air Force and the Salvation Army.

Ms. Bergman suggests that parents ease into this transition. A few weeks before you return to work, try separating yourself from your child occasionally. Put her in group play, a babysitting co-op, or even in a cooperative preschool, where another parent is always present.

Dr. Little adds, "When you leave your child for the first time, don't sneak away. Always tell your child when you are leaving. Don't get them occupied and walk away. That hurts their trust level."

Because children between ages 2 and 6 have a limited concept of time, she says, it's good to provide concrete examples for them, such as, "I'll pick you up after lunch or after play period."

Dr. Little also suggests leaving children with reminders of a parent, like putting a picture of mom or dad in their lunch box. Or letting them keep a favorite key chain or stuffed animal, for example, to help them adjust.

## ARE OUR CHILDREN SAFE?

As we learn to let go, our children become part of the changing process. They are forced to adjust to new schools, daycare, and even coming home alone. As we adapt to change, how do we know if we are forcing our children to grow up too soon?

Natalie, 42, recalls coming home from work and seeing her 9-year-old son, Jonathan, sitting alone on the porch, with streaks of dried tears down his face. Two boys had threatened him, and he couldn't get into his house because he'd lost his key.

Three months of being a "latchkey" child were enough for Jonathan. Although he enjoyed his freedom, his days were difficult. He got chased by dogs, pelted by rain, threatened by older boys, bored by television. And he never finished his homework.

Even though Jonathan had asked his mother to let him come home alone after school, after a few weeks he admitted: "Coming home from school [alone] is not what it's cracked up to be."

Jonathan's situation is similar to that of thousands of school children whose parents work. In "Latchkey Children: Statistics Unlocked," the *Washington Times* reports that 14 percent of children ages 5 to 12 spend an average of one hour home alone after school, which is the equivalent of 3.5 million children.

When children have been away all day, they need to return to an environment where they receive emotional support from a main caretaker. Younger children don't receive the proper emotional connection when they are home alone. Watching TV or playing video games doesn't give them what they need.

Emotionally, children left in self-care may put up a brave front, but they are still frightened. Also, leaving a child alone or in charge of younger siblings probably puts too much pressure on them.

## TOO MUCH TOO SOON

As we begin "letting go" of our past lives and attachments, Dr. David Elkind, professor of child study at Tufts University, warns divorced parents to not "hurry" their children into adult responsibilities too soon. "When a woman finds herself alone and responsible for a family, the initial reaction may be one of shock and panic. For one thing, by having custody of the children, the woman now feels she must fill the role of mother and father," says Dr. Elkind, author of *The Hurried Child* (Addison-Wesley, 1988). Because of this, solo parenting is more difficult, since there's no one to share the load with or lean on in time of stress.

Dr. Elkind warns parents about the temptation to use children as a go-between in conflicts with your ex. It's also tempting to confide in your child about problems with your boss, financial difficulties, or your new boyfriend. When a child lends a sympathetic ear, he or she may be offering what the mother needs. "Unfortunately, though, it is by no means clear that this is what the child needs," Elkind says.

As 5-year-old Deana tells Dr. Elkind in session, "I like Mommy's friend who smells nice but I don't like the furry one that smells bad. Sometimes," she says nervously, "I wish she wouldn't ask me [about him]."

## LETTING GO DURING THE HOLIDAYS

For some, the fun and laughter of the holidays are a painful reminder of losses—the loss of a husband, a family, or our dreams.

But there is hope.

After her husband's airplane crash, Verdell Davis began trying to find meaning in the tragedy. In an effort to wrestle with her thoughts and feelings and to better understand herself, she began a journal.

"The words became the wings from my life experience," she says. "As I went through the grief and loss, trying to put my life together again, I needed the words to make sense of my emotions."

From these writings came her book *Let Me Grieve, But Not Forever*, describing her journey from loss to recovery and how she learned to live independently. Ms. Davis describes the loneliness that crept in after the accident, saying, "It was like an octopus with eight long tentacles, wrapped around me; and the harder I fought, the tighter it squeezed."

During these difficult times, she turned to other widows whose husbands had died in the accident. A shared grief is special, she says. "I don't know how I could have made it without their support. We called each other daily or, if we had a rough time, in the middle of the night."

The first Christmas after the accident, the four wives gathered at a favorite family hunting lodge. With their children, they commemorated their husbands' lives and celebrated their friendship.

"My husband's airplane crash made no sense to me," adds Ms. Davis. "At that time, I had two choices. I could turn away from God in anger or I could allow the experience to open me up to new opportunities."

## FREEDOM TO BE ME

On her 50th birthday, Ms. Davis's children surprised her by renting a red convertible for the day. The gift had a special meaning. In her marriage, when days became tedious, she often jokingly reminded her husband that "for my mid-life crisis I want a red convertible."

In her book she describes her pleasure.

I laughed and cried as I drove that rented red convertible around with the top down . . . my children had no way of knowing that they were giving me back my life. That red convertible had to be returned, but not the things it gave me: the freedom to dream, the daring to live life to the fullest, the permission to enjoy the moment, in spite of its temporary nature. . . . With that birthday gift came a new way of relating to the life that lay in front of me. I was beginning to reach out toward life with open arms. . . . Time by itself doesn't heal all wounds. Unless we deal with the loss, it does not heal. My children, friends, and other surviving wives gave me guidance and direction when I needed it. With their encouragement, I was able to travel the journey of grief, a journey which I found has a destination.

## LETTING GO OF ANGER

Are you having difficulty letting go of your past? Are you discovering twists and turns in your "journey"? Are you obsessed with vivid memories? Memories you'd like to forget? Like many widows and divorcees, the past sometimes consumes us.

**Beth, brand-new breadwinner.** After her divorce, Beth was consumed with anger. During her marriage, she'd quit school to work and put her husband through law school. Now, she was getting no alimony and meager child support. After being a stay-at-home mom for 10 years, she was now forced to become the breadwinner. Although enraged, she tried to push the anger from her mind. She knew it was preventing her from moving forward. In an attempt to let go of her resentment, Beth gathered her husband's personal items and packed them away in the garage so he could pick them up and take them to his new home.

As Beth looked around the garage, she was amazed. After two years of separation, there were still remnants of her ex-husband everywhere. Like an angry child, Beth tossed his belongings into a large cardboard box, silently hoping they'd be destroyed. Running shoes. Baseball glove. Fraternity pictures. Law degree. Even an autographed picture of Nixon, which her husband had proudly displayed on his desk before the Watergate scandal.

It wasn't until she reached for his cowboy hat and boots, that she froze, her hand lifted in mid-air.

Beside the boots stood a dusty picture of a young couple standing next to an old pickup truck in the middle of a muddy pasture. The couple held two long-neck beers, laughing into the camera. It was hard to believe that this couple was Beth and her ex, Sam. Their innocence was touching.

Suddenly, Beth realized the sweetness of their life together. Her shy husband, who communicated with difficulty, loved the outdoors. It was there, on the weekends in the country, that they found each other. By mending fences or caring for their cattle, they shared something special. And it was while camping out under the stars that they conceived their first child.

This land they affectionately called "the ranch" wasn't much. Certainly not by Texas standards. Just a few acres of hard-scrabble land filled with bois d'arc trees and boasting six cows. But to Beth and Sam this was paradise, the beginning of new life. And one they shared together.

As Beth gazed at the picture, her anger dissipated. She realized their happiness had been limited, but powerful. They'd created two loving children, and, in many ways, a beautiful life together.

In the months that followed, Beth began to put her past behind her. The last days of her marriage lost their bitterness.

Maybe she married too young. Maybe they needed

more weekends on the ranch. Maybe they were too different. Who knows? Their marriage may have been an unfortunate failure, but it had its moments. Precious moments.

After months of struggle, Beth was able to let go.

Just like Beth, you may soon realize that there is an end in sight. You may feel better now that he's moved out and started divorce proceedings. Someday your marriage will be in the past. And the anguish will be a distant memory.

As you try new things, meet new people, and sample new adventures in life, you realize just how capable you are. And how worthy you are of *a better life*. In a few months, you may happily report that you can buy your own car, pay your rent or mortgage, and care for your children. *All on your own.*

And you may discover *a new you*. Someone who won't compromise. Who likes herself. And who has new hope for the future. *Your* future.

## CHAPTER 2 REVIEW: LETTING GO PAVES THE WAY TO A HAPPY NEW FUTURE

- **Acknowledge and accept your grief.**
- **Express grief and react to it.** Memorialize the loss with a ritual. Light a candle, make a collage of photos, write a poem, or cut out scraps of material from the person's clothes and make a pillow. Even if the loss is painful, find happy thoughts to recall.
- **Find positive outlets for emotions.** Pursue a passion like a political or environmental cause, a

new career, or paint a picture, or write a book, and more.

- **Guide your children as they let go.** Whether entering a new school or adjusting to a new home, each transition should be introduced gradually. Step by step, children learn to succeed independently.

- **Alleviate a child's fear.** By putting a picture of mom in your child's lunchbox, or letting her take a key chain or a stuffed animal, you will ease the anxiety of starting a new school or day care experience.

- **Leaving your child home alone.** Make sure your child is developmentally ready for this sometimes overwhelming experience. Experts suggest children under 12 should not be left home alone.

- **Don't rush your child.** As you let go, be sensitive to your child's needs. Don't rush him into inappropriate situations, like discussing your new boyfriend, criticizing your ex, or discussing details about finances.

- **Letting go through the holidays.** Reach out to others. Let them take care of you. Don't take on Christmas dinner. Let someone else be responsible.

- **Lean on friends.** Let them nurture and guide you during the grief journey, which does have an end ultimately.

- **Learn to let go.** As you try new things, meet new people and sample new adventures in life, you'll let go of the past and discover a NEW YOU!

## Chapter Three

# the challenge of uncoupling

It is a warm summer evening in Bridgeport, Connecticut. Lightening bugs dance in the dark, and the air smells of honeysuckle. As the couples finish their bridge game, their soft laughter carries over the yard to the neighbors nearby.

Sitting on her screened porch, Annette hears the laughter, and she responds with a pang of regret. The couples enjoying the evening are some of her closest friends, but she wasn't invited to their bridge game. Since her husband died a few months ago, she is no longer included in their get-togethers. Now she knows why: she is single. They are couples. And she's not part of their world anymore.

## IT'S A COUPLED WORLD

Like many women who find themselves suddenly single, Annette realizes she no longer fits into a coupled world. Dinner parties, bridge, tennis, and travel packages, all are geared toward couples. Now that she isn't part of a couple, she feels odd, like a "third wheel."

"After Harry died, I needed my old friends," explains Annette. "But I could feel them beginning to pull away." After a friend's husband dropped by and offered to fix Annette's water heater, the wife stopped calling Annette.

"I was surprised," replied Annette, "because we'd been friends for years, but I think she was threatened by the fact that I was single."

This feeling is common, experts say. Friendships are heavily impacted by death and divorce. And adjusting to a friend's death or divorce is a learning process. As busy as things are today, it's often easier to avoid the situation than to deal with it.

In his book *Rebuilding When Your Relationship Ends* (Impact, 1992), author Bruce Fisher says that as you go through a divorce, you may experience a sense of "not knowing" resembling a state of limbo. In divorce, there is a legal as well as an emotional separation, he adds, but society is still not as accepting of the divorcee. She's still regarded as a threat to other married couples. Some feel divorce may be "catching."

In the process of uncoupling, the loss of old friends can be painful. In the upscale neighborhood where Lee, 41, a divorcee lived, she noticed the wives of wealthy men have the greatest adjustment to make. "If women are economically dependent on their husbands, they seem to suffer the most," she explains. If their husbands make most of the money, then the husbands often control the actions of their friends. The men provide box seats to local sports events, a membership to the tennis club, tables at the finest restaurants, and leads for business transactions. "Unfortunately, the wives are dropped from social circles," Lee says. "When men have the most economic power, they also have social power, and their wives are left with nothing."

## MEETING THE CHALLENGE OF UNCOUPLING—A SUCCESS STORY

Uncoupling has never been a problem for character actress Anne Haney. In 1980, after her husband died of kidney disease, she couldn't resist the temptation to change her life.

At the age of 45, Anne left her hometown of Atlanta and moved to Hollywood, leaving her community, her friends and her family, without looking back. She had no idea if she'd make it. But she figured this was her last chance to pursue her dream: acting. After leasing her home, she set out for the West Coast with the name of an agent tucked in her pocket.

Where did she get so much moxy? "I'd waited long enough," says Anne. "Besides, I always wanted to play with the big boys. I am, at heart, competitive."

While spending her married life in Atlanta and raising her daughter Melissa, she devoted herself to being a homemaker. "I was a lovely faculty wife," she says. "We made ambrosia salad. We did good works. We played a lot of bridge. But I was beginning to cook those three meals a day with my teeth clenched. Feminism was hitting, and I started looking around for other things to do."

Then came acting. In 1970, Anne began working in

commercials and local theater. The next step was dinner theater, where she played the maid in Noel Coward's *Fallen Angels;* Dorothy Lamour was the lead. At the same time, she began landing supporting roles in movie and TV shows cast out of Atlanta. She got her Screen Actors Guild card and joined the American Federation of TV and Radio Artists.

As her husband neared retirement, they agreed to move to Hollywood to give Anne the chance to try her hand at acting, but then he became ill. After his death, the Memphis, Tennessee, native continued to pursue her dream.

A month after arriving in Los Angeles, she had an agent. A month after that, she was working. "They were happy to see a new face, a new old face," explains Anne, who plays character parts such as wrinkled grandmothers, crusty old women, or middle-aged secretaries. Resembling the actress Jessica Tandy, she has guest-starred on *Murder One, The Client, NYPD Blue,* and in numerous movies. She played with Jim Carrey in *Liar, Liar.* She was the family-court supervisor in 1993's *Mrs. Doubtfire,* and she was Michael Douglas's secretary in *The American President.* Other films she's appeared in are *Psycho, Mother, Forces of Nature,* and *Midnight in the Garden of Good and Evil.*

How did she make it in one of the nation's toughest businesses? "I wrote a lot of thank-you notes," she says laughing. Ms. Haney is considered by producers to be money in the bank—meaning she's easy to work with. "I learn my lines. I hit my marks, and I don't make trouble on the set. There are 10 ladies who can do equally well, who are doing the same kind of parts I'm doing, and we sort of swap around," she says.

At one time, though, Anne wondered if she'd ever make it.

Growing up the South, she wasn't given the chance to be an actress. Anne points out that in the South, women tended to have few choices. "In my day, acting was not something a lady does. We were raised to be wives and mothers."

But when her husband died, she broke those rules. "I left my home, and all that was familiar to me, struck out on my own—and I loved it," she says. "I was ready—growing up, I never imagined I'd have this opportunity."

Today, she enjoys her days off gardening in her beautiful home in Studio City. She's bought her own house and pays cash for her cars. "And I love acting—it's a wonderful way to spend the last third of my life."

## SOCIAL STATUS CHANGES

An established commercial realtor, Lee was able to avoid a financial setback after her divorce because of her professional success. But she still felt like a failure in her personal life. "It took me a long time to trust my instincts and my judgment again," she says.

Uncoupling causes a multitude of losses, says Sheila Madigan Levatino, a therapist and grief consultant. "There's the loss of a spouse, the breakup of your family and in-laws, and finances. And if someone is forced to sell her home, she loses her neighborhood and community as well." In short, some women lose an entire lifestyle and social status. Jennifer's husband was the deacon at her church. Now, she's embarrassed to attend church, because she worries about what others are saying about the divorce. Although she's been a member for 15 years, she feels out of place, because her husband still has a position of power within the church. The thought of sitting across the aisle from him on Sunday mornings makes her feel uncomfortable.

## HOW TO HANDLE HOLIDAY PARTIES

A year after the death of Mary Lou's husband, a friend invited her to a Christmas party, urging her to bring a date. After being married for over 20 years, Mary Lou didn't know anyone who was single. "All our friends are couples," she explained.

After much thought, she decided to go alone. When she walked into the party, she was overwhelmed with fear. As her sharp heels clicked against the oak floor, she seemed like the only one in the room. One by one, the people turned and stared. For a split second, Mary Lou wanted to make a hasty exit. But she stayed.

Her husband had been an outgoing man who was always the life of the party. She was used to him getting most of the attention. But tonight was different. Warmed by the wine, she began to relax and listen to the people around her. She was surprised by how people responded. They laughed at her jokes. They listened to her stories. And they complimented her new outfit.

As the evening whizzed by, Mary Lou forgot about the time. And she forgot about being nervous. It was the first time in years that she'd been out alone. "I was amazed that I had a personality of my own, that I could make it by myself," she says. "This made me happy and I began to bloom."

Months later, Mary Lou joined a gourmet cooking club and won a blue ribbon at the state fair for her favorite pasta recipe. She was on her way. She got a new job, made new friends, and felt good about herself. Although she missed her husband's companionship, she was thrilled to discover a new serenity.

Lee, the realtor, is another case in point. After her divorce, she solved the uncoupling problem by asking her gay friend to be her date to parties. "It was a perfect match," she says. "I wanted to go out, but I didn't want to get serious about anyone. I felt safe with John."

When you are going through a loss, you need one or two good friends to support you. "Preferably a childhood friend," says Ms. Levatino, a therapist, who conducts grief groups for the American Society of Psychologists. "You need someone in your corner. Someone who will be honest with you."

Uncoupling poses a challenge, especially at parties where you are forced to show up without a partner. In order to prepare for this occasion, Ms. Levatino suggests that you select an escort, whether it's a formal date or just a friend. "You need to plan who will be your anchor or security blanket at the party," she says. "And don't forget to rehearse what you're going to do when you get there." She suggests asking yourself: Who will I talk to at the party? How long will I stay? What will I do if my spouse is there? "Treat yourself nicely," says Ms. Levatino, who suggests setting a minimal, achievable goal at the party, such as planning to stay only 30 to 40 minutes. If you make it to 25 minutes and can't take it anymore, then leave.

## OCEANS OF EMOTIONS

When you're in the throes of a divorce, it's like a storm at sea. You need someone to help you walk through it. During a loss, mood swings are high and low. Many women feel anger in a way they've never felt before. Women who are used to being "nice girls" may feel out of control. They may not know how to handle this fresh rage.

Anger tempts us to throw ketchup on our ex, to key his car, or worse. Or you may be tempted to wear a back-less dress to a church holiday party, just to spite him. If you find yourself resorting to adolescent behavior, try channeling your rage into a physical activity, like using a punching bag or joining a yoga class. Or you may write your ex a letter you never mail, or take a drive in the country and scream as loud as you can.

After her divorce, Lee got sick and came down with a 103-degree fever. "Fortunately, I had girlfriends I could depend on," she said. "I wasn't afraid to call them, saying, 'I don't need to be fixed up with anybody, but I need you, and I need you now.'"

## FACING ROLE CHANGES

With women who have lost a spouse, sometimes the smallest tasks are insurmountable. Walking into the senior center without a companion is very difficult, says Debbie Rhinehart-Young, a social worker for a wellness center for the elderly. For those who have been married for a long time, there is a ritual of coming to the senior center each week with their spouse. When their spouse is gone, they must grieve over the loss.

But grieving is not enough. Learning to live alone also means learning new tasks. Women over the age of 65 may not be prepared to assume tasks normally handled by their husbands. Like shoveling snow, putting gas in the car and changing the oil, hiring a man to trim the trees, or handling the finances.

Many members of the older generation didn't have to do these things, and some women are not willing or able to assume these responsibilities. Sarah, 72, was perfectly happy to depend on her husband's financial adviser. When her son pointed out that her stocks were not making any money, she chose to ignore his advice. Her financial adviser was like an authority figure to her. Her husband trusted him and she felt comfortable with him, too—even though she was losing hundreds of dollars a month.

"Sometimes older women tend to turn over authority to male father-figures," explained Ms. Rhinehart-Young. "Because these individuals represent people they feel safe with, they're reluctant to change."

## THE UNCERTAINTIES OF UNCOUPLING

Whether you're 35 or 85, uncoupling breeds insecurity and uncertainty. Rage is spilling out everywhere. Women are faced with major financial decisions which affect their livelihood. And these decisions must often be made quickly. With this onslaught of demands, some of us cope by going into denial. We make excuses. We look the other way, as we ignore our debts and avoid making financial decisions. Our lack of financial security undermines everything else.

In the first year after your divorce or your spouse's death, you may be faced with selling your home and moving. You may realize that you need to return to work. You may face spending the holidays alone, or without the family support you once had. You may also face an empty chair at the dining room table.

How do you prepare for this emptiness?

Let's take the holidays. Try celebrating in a new way. Have a Mexican food feast. Break a piñata. Pass out balloons. And light a candle for your loved one.

If you're used to spending the holidays in the snow, go to the beach and lay out in the sun. If you're used to turkey with all the trimmings, try something simple. Order a pizza and share a bottle of wine with friends. Build a fire and watch your favorite movies on video.

If you're used to spending the holidays with your ex-husband's sister, make other plans. Or, instead of spending the holidays alone, arrange to eat with friends or celebrate with your extended family. If you're tired of cooking, ask your grown children to make the holiday dinner at your house or theirs.

## UNCOUPLING WITH CHILDREN

At last, your divorce is finalized. Visitation, education, insurance, and support are all taken care of. Case closed.

But don't get too relaxed. Your divorce decree may not be as airtight as you might think. Did you know that the non-custodial and support-paying parent has the right, at

## COMMON FEELINGS FACING DIVORCEES

- **Fear of the future.** It comes in all the ways you can imagine. There's the fear concerning your safety and security. Fear of being alone. Fear of the dark. Fear of making financial decisions. Fear of destitution. Fear of attack. Fear of victimization.
- **Destructive anger.** It takes the form of revenge, rage, blame, violence, or feeling out of control. Anger keeps you stuck in the past and connected to your ex.
- **Losing control.** Do what it takes to regain control over your life. Get professional help, go to school, learn new skills, go to support groups, nurture yourself.
- **Negative thoughts.** Wipe these thoughts away by concentrating on what you've got, not what you've lost.

SOURCE: **AARP**

any time, to open up issues of child support and relationship with very little cause? Your ex may be able to alter the amounts paid on support. And with a clever lawyer, he can revisit everything you struggled and fought for during the divorce. And this can happen no matter how many years ago that struggle occurred.

And what about the children? Did you know that your

children also feel the stress of uncoupling? They miss their aunts, uncles, cousins, and other relatives, especially their grandparents. Because of the special bond they share, encourage your children to stay in contact with their grandparents. One way is to phone saying, "we have a present for you. Can we come by?"

Have you sold your home? Are your children living in a different neighborhood? Are they attending a different school? Encourage them to call on old friends, or to send Grandpa a birthday present or card. Although children may not show it, they're also grieving over their losses. Not only do they miss their dad reading to them at night or tucking them in, they may also miss seeing their other relatives on a regular basis.

Surprisingly, even grown children have difficulty with the uncoupling process. They may face spending the holiday with their father and his new girlfriend. Or they may face sharing the holiday in a new setting with new rituals.

Less than a year after her mother's death, Cindy's father remarried and sold her childhood home. Within a few months, Cindy, 38, lost the opportunity to celebrate and share family memories in a familiar place. No longer could she imagine smelling her mother's fresh-baked cranberry pie, or the sight of colorful packages under the tree by the bay window. No longer could she soak in the memories of where she grew up.

Bruce Drobeck, a marriage and family counselor, says these situations are common. "Children have a hard time realizing that their parents have a life outside the family circle," he says. "There's a fantasy that our parents will al-

## COMMON FEELINGS FACING THE NEWLY WIDOWED

You will probably share most or all of the same feelings as divorced women. In addition, the newly widowed may have other feelings that are unique due to the loss of a spouse.

- **Mental obstacles to overcome.** There's the fear of being unwelcome in a coupled world. Fear of going crazy because of mental confusion brought on by grief. Fear of a mental slow-down.
- **Self-esteem.** It's not uncommon to feel a loss of self-identity and self-esteem. Suddenly, you may be unable to determine your role in life.

Having to deal with all of these varied, complicated, intertwined feelings, you may want to start over. It's a natural reaction, because many of us feel if we leave our home or old neighborhood, we'll also move away from our pain.

Be careful. Sometimes, moving away only replaces old pain with a new set of painful challenges.

SOURCE: AARP

ways look after us." He points out that it's hard for children, even adult children, to let go of their parents and see them as independent adults. It forces the children to redefine their own roles.

**WHEN PARENTS SPLIT**

- Data indicate that women and children are at elevated risk for violence during the process of and after separation.
- Seventy-three percent of battered women seeking emergency medical services have recently undergone a separation.
- Fifty to seventy percent of men who abuse their wives or partners also abuse their children.
- In 1992, 354,100 children were reported abducted by family members who violated custody agreements or decrees. Most victims were children ages 2–11.

SOURCE: 1994 Child Safety Act

## FAMILY DYNAMICS BEGIN TO CHANGE

In the first year after death or divorce, everyone is trying to figure out who they are. The family dynamics change, throwing everyone out of kilter. We need to prepare for this occurrence. Although you may now be facing life alone, you do not need to be lonely. Attending holiday celebrations, social gatherings, bridge groups, church services, classes, or parties will most likely seem different. However, you can gain newer and richer experiences from them. Try networking with others going through a similar experience. Share a holiday meal with a certain group. Enroll in a painting class. Attend a special worship service. Join the symphony league. Volunteer at a homeless shelter. Or throw a "divorce party" for your friends.

At first, learning to live alone isn't easy. Your life has changed. Either by choice or not, you've discarded your traditional family. Now, you must learn to begin anew. In time, you will learn to cherish your time alone. There's no worrying about calling home when you stay out late. You don't need to be making dinner at a certain time. No rush to grocery shop on Wednesday. You can wait until Friday. You may love living your life without interruption, deadlines, rules, or expectations.

## THE ANN RICHARDS STORY

When she lost the race against George W. Bush in 1994, former Governor Ann Richards didn't spend but "two minutes mourning the fact." Leaving politics forced her to pursue new interests. "I looked forward to learning new things, starting a new life," she says. And indeed she did start over. Divorced after being married for 30 years, she sold her home and threw herself into a new life.

The challenge of learning to live alone, Ms. Richards admits, "is getting over the initial trauma, because you assume that you are going to live the rest of your life with someone.

"In time, you realize that the most important person you need to live with is yourself. We [women] invest so much time in the well-being and comfort of others, that we often ignore the nurturing that we need for ourselves.

"I love being single," she concludes. "I love my life. I can't imagine it any other way. In two weeks, I'm taking a trip to Russia with my daughter . . . and I couldn't do that if I were married."

## CHANGING CULTURAL EXPECTATIONS

Okay, you're ready to start a new life. You're full of expectation. But what about the "tapes you keep hearing," like "you've ruined your life," or "the children will suffer," or "you'll never find a man who loved you like your first husband."

As Ann Richards says, these messages were created by people who were worried about their own lives, not yours. As we experience loss, it's important to realize that we come from a culture where "living alone" is frowned upon. Are people trying to find you a partner? They may not want you to live a life different from theirs. Or they may feel that your living alone is somewhat eccentric. Women are meant to spend their lives with someone. Parents. Children. Brothers. Sisters. Uncles. Aunts. Cousins. And—in recent years, with reluctant acceptance—significant others.

Being paired off is normal, people say. Everything else is considered a transition or unnatural. As young girls, we're programmed to "get along with others," to build relationships, to sustain life, to be the nurturers. We are told that we have mysterious powers. The power to calm. The power to love. The power to heal. The power to provide peace. The power to create a band of loyal followers.

In spite of this endless rhetoric, more and more people are living alone. A little more than 12 percent of the adult population now lives alone, up from 7 percent 20 years ago. And what about the women? Middle-aged women are the fastest-growing singles group.

As women learn to live alone, they find it's a learned process, often difficult at the beginning. As the women gain confidence and adapt new skills, they often find themselves in a "new skin," one that brings comfort each day.

**Blanche, 63.** Her husband committed suicide by driving their car off a cliff in northern California. At the age of 63, Blanche was left with no automobile and no insurance. She had never worked outside the home, and she was filled with anger.

With time, though, she began her life anew. She joined a church in her neighborhood and began counseling with a priest, who helped her work through her anger. She also took a clerical job at the local university, which led to a higher-paying recruiting job. A nature-lover, she then joined a hiking club and began enjoying camp-outs and outdoor excursions with new friends.

**Freda, 65, is another widow.** Married to a Detroit policeman, she cared for their four children while he handled the finances and the major household repairs. In addition to not working full-time, Freda had never learned to drive. A few months after his death, she took a driving course because she wanted to become more independent. The thrill of passing her driving test gave her a boost of confidence. She excitedly called her son and told him she was going to meet him for lunch at his lake house.

## PROTECTING KIDS FROM THEIR PARENTS

Sometimes uncoupling turns into a brawl between spouses. If that's your problem, the following story shows how to solve it.

As young police officer Michael Wood, 36, pulls into the driveway, he nervously checks his watch. It's 5:45 P.M. He is on time. He has to be, or the divorced father's first visit in four months with his 9-year-old daughter and his 4-year-old son will be canceled. Just 15 minutes earlier, his ex-wife had dropped them off so the warring parents could avoid contact.

As Wood approaches a tree-shaded home in the historic section of Austin, Texas, he notices his children drawing with chalk on the sidewalk. When they see their father, their smiles are hesitant, but the warmth of their eyes gives them away. "Daddy!" they say, as he gathers them in his arms.

Welcome to the Kids Exchange, one of 80 such "neutral zones" for children and parents that have proliferated nationwide along with the rise in domestic violence. In 1993 alone, 1,299 children were killed by their parents in the U.S.A. Says Linda Hahn, the director of family court services in Dallas County, Texas, "With the growing outbreak of sexual and physical abuse of children, there is a crying need for supervised visitation centers."

These drop-off centers provide havens where children of divorce can safely visit the "non-custodial" parent. Some centers provide a safe haven for children whose parents are accused of mental or physical abuse or neglect, or whose parents are involved in custody disputes. Some also provide a place where foster kids can meet with their estranged parents. Without such visitation centers, kids often are exchanged in parking lots or fast-food restaurants, places where violence often escalates.

The centers also help children keep in contact with non-custodial parents impaired by substance abuse, mental illness, or mental retardation. "It's still important for children's development to remain in contact with that parent," says Rob Straus, the director of The Meeting Place in Cambridge, Massachussetts. "The child wants the abuse to stop, but he doesn't necessarily want to lose that parent."

Joanne Karolzak, president of the Visitation Network, an advocacy group in Tuscon, Arizona, calls such centers the "burgeoning social service" of the future.

The Kids Exchange in Austin is helping the Herrington family. Because of a court decree, Leslie Herrington, a machine technician for the Colorado River Authority, was ordered to cease all communication with his former wife and to use the Kids Exchange when he picked up his 11-year-old son for weekend visitations.

"Kids Exchange has provided me with a neutral zone where I may pick up my son and drop him off," says Herrington, 34. "It allows me to be more relaxed, because I know there will not be a confrontation between his mother and me."

After months of being defensive about the program, Herrington now praises it. "I realized that Kids Exchange was not there to just monitor me. They were there to make sure the visits with my son went smoothly. They served as an effective mediator between my wife and me."

The approach also has worked for Austin's Michael Wood. Wood, who was accused of physically abusing one of his kids—allegations that were later dropped—says he felt like a "criminal" when he met his children during supervised visits at the Kids Exchange. "Here I was—a respected police office, and I was ashamed of being forced to use this service," he says. Now, after positive reports, he is allowed to use the program for exchanges, picking up his children and taking them to his home for weekend visits.

"Now that we don't confront each other when we exchange our children, our anger is defused and the allegations [by his ex] have stopped," he says.

**FOR YOUR INFORMATION**

Do you want to avoid angry confrontations with your ex in front of your child? Contact the New York Society for the Prevention of Cruelty to Children (NYSPCC) to ask for the Supervised Visitation Network in your area. Call (800) 447-7220.

## CHAPTER 3 REVIEW: UNCOUPLING CAN HAVE A HAPPY ENDING

- **Choose supportive friends.** Adjusting to a divorce or death is a learning process. Establish contacts with friends who have endured a loss. They'll be more comforting to you.
- **Too many changes?** When you're faced with multiple changes in your life, nurture yourself. Read a book. Take a bubble bath. Have lunch with a friend. Plan down time for yourself.
- **Handling holidays.** During holiday time, try something different. Establish a new ritual. Make an altar to a departed loved one, consisting of mementos, pictures, poems, or motivational messages.
- **Party protocol.** Attending a holiday party? Go with a male or female friend who'll leave when you're ready. Don't force yourself to stay for the whole party. Twenty to thirty minutes will do.
- **Establish boundaries.** Learn to say no to well-meaning friends, attorneys, or financial consultants who insist they know what's best for you.
- **Cutting the clutter.** Cut the clutter from your home. Go through closets, chests, or desk drawers and separate your items into piles marked "throw away," "save," and "give to charity." You'll save time and money if you simplify your life.
- **How to handle kids.** When your children react negatively to the uncoupling process, assure them that though "daddy's not here every day, we'll always be a family."

- **Protect your independence.** Make your own rules. If babysitting's not your thing, say so!
- **Go it alone.** Don't be afraid to walk to the senior center, attend a party, or eat out alone. You'd be surprised at how easy it is to meet others when you're alone.
- **Exercise, exercise, exercise.** Exercise at least 20 minutes a day. Walk, jog, jump rope, hike, bicycle—every day. If you don't have time, try breaking it up into 10-minute increments. Just remember to move. Push your grocery cart around the parking lot. Climb stairs at work. Walk your dog. Lift weights. Try yoga. It all works to lift your spirits!

## Chapter Four

# to relocate or
# stay put

Jean, 42, thought she had her life under control. Five months after her divorce, she took a job in another city, Minneapolis, and rented a house for herself and her three children. In order to make the transition easier, she flew in ahead of her children. Then she moved their favorite furniture and stuffed animals into each of their new bedrooms, carefully arranging her children's books and toys just the way they were before.

She was determined to make each child feel at home, whether ensuring the safety of her daughters' canopy bed and soccer ball or her son's CDs and videos. In fact, she spent so much time worrying about her children's anxiety over moving that she forgot all about herself.

Weeks after the move, she began to oversleep, causing her children to be chronically late to school. She was used to having her husband help with the children. Now, she found the challenge of being a single mother overwhelming. In addition to adjusting to a new job, she was saddled with packing lunches, preparing meals, carpooling, and overseeing homework—all alone. Normally a detail-oriented person who was good at math, Jean knew she was in trouble when she began to rely on her 13-year-old to balance her checkbook and pay the utility bills.

## RUNNING FAST, RUNNING SCARED

After a loss, you may find yourself hurrying here and there and going nowhere. Fast. You may feel constantly fearful as well.

At this stage, many women long to make a change, any change. As in the movie *Thelma and Louise*, you may want to switch jobs, sell the house, pack up the Suburban, and head off into the sunset, leaving your troubles behind.

Some women succeed in doing this. Some don't.

Take Marge, 63, for instance. After her husband died, the silence became deafening. She missed his whistling in the morning. She missed his chatting about the news. She even missed his grumbling about the cold weather. And there were the silent, symbolic things that got to her, too. His overcoat hanging in the hall. His aftershave lotion staring at her when she opened the bathroom cabinet. Even his pile of magazines stashed in the corner spoke to her, without making a sound. These items were not only difficult for her to see or touch, they were also impossible for her to let go of.

From the polished oak cabinets to the handmade bookshelves in the study, Marge was constantly reminded of her husband's love of woodworking. Those reminders of the gentle hands she longed to have hold her constantly kept him in her heart.

Marge could almost hear her husband's footsteps. And one night, she thought she saw his shadow move across the hall. Frequently she felt his presence in the room, especially the bedroom.

Marge didn't understand why she kept searching for her husband everywhere. He was gone. She didn't understand why she felt so uneasy in her own home. It wasn't natural, but that's the way it was. Finally, within a couple of months of her husband's death, Katherine wanted to move.

## ARE YOU EMOTIONALLY READY?

After a death or divorce, you may feel like your life is spinning out of control. But before you make any major decisions about moving or finances, think things out *rationally*. Use your head, not your heart.

### TOO MUCH TOO SOON

Harriet, at age 61, was determined to make a change. She thought moving would alleviate her feelings of despair. After moving to the West Coast to be near her daughter and grandchildren, though, her world began to unravel.

With her daughter working full time and the children busy in after-school activities, she rarely saw them until the weekends. Her apartment was cramped and couldn't hold all her belongings, and she was unable to drive in the city.

Instead of spending leisure time with her daughter and grandchildren, their visits were rushed. Everyone was in a hurry. Harriet was amazed to find that she spent endless hours in her apartment waiting, waiting for her daughter to call. She felt like she was losing control over her life.

She is not alone. The number of retirement-age people moving from state to state increased 63 percent from 1982 to 1992. "And many of these people make tremendous adjustments when they move to be near their children," says Pat Hatchell, who heads a senior wellness center. Women who move are leaving behind a strong network of neighbors, friends, church members, bridge group, or even their hair stylist, people they have known for years.

Chloe, 65, who managed and owned apartment dwellings, fell into this category. After losing her husband, she longed to be near her daughter, her only child. Still whirling from her loss, she quickly sold her real estate holdings to the highest bidder, packed her belongings, and moved. Unfortunately, she left her independence behind.

Without her business, she felt a tremendous loss of pride, as well as a loss of income. The move also marked the beginning of painful arthritis, which continued throughout her life. Eventually, Chloe moved back to her home town.

## WOMEN OVER 65 WHO MOVE MAY GET IN OVER THEIR HEADS

Relocating is difficult for women 65 and over. They are more fragile, says Pat Hatchell, because they lose their support system. "When you are not a couple anymore, you no longer have someone to share your experiences or feelings with," she says. "And you have to prepare yourself for going to the senior center alone, or eating out alone. If you're not in the workplace or a member of the PTA, you must reorganize your life and find a way to rebuild social contacts."

And what if you're really up in years? According to geriatric care professionals, people over 75 may suffer from relocation stress syndrome, causing feelings of loneliness, abandonment, or confusion. Depending on your age and physical condition, it takes three to six months to adjust to a new living situation.

## PAIN IN PARTING

Phyllis Smith, owner of a moving company for seniors, agrees. The hardest part of moving is parting with material things, she says.

"Holiday dinners served with a special set of dishes, vacation mementos, or a comfy chair can all represent precious memories," says Ms. Smith, who moves up to 15 elderly families a month.

In order to alleviate the confusion of relocating, she advises that individuals sort or sell items that have accumulated for dozens of years *before the move*. For example, one of her widow clients had a garage sale where she sold big-ticket items, such as her husband's piano and pool table. She got rid of books, furniture, and tools, too. She then decided which remaining items were to be moved, stored, or discarded.

Senior citizens face an emotional journey when saying

goodbye to a beloved home and possessions, geriatric care experts say. However, older adults can avoid feelings of depression and anxiety if they plan ahead and make their own decisions concerning their move.

Ruth, 79, made such a decision after her husband, Charles, died of stomach cancer. She sold her home and moved into a nearby retirement center to live in a more "protected" environment.

Although sudden, this move was *her* decision. And it suggests that older people need to plan where they are going, and where they'll end up. "You better make a move before you're helpless," says Ruth.

Before she moved, she also sat down with her children and expressed her feelings to them about death and change. "It's no taboo subject," she says. "They knew all along what I wanted to do."

## ARE YOU READY TO MAKE A MOVE?

Whether we're 35 or 85, loss affects us the same way. And our homes can remind of us that loss. Physical reminders like an overcoat, an umbrella, or a rose garden can bring our partner to life, then, just as quickly, tear him away from us. Even if we've gone through a painful divorce, we sometimes hope that the sweet man we first married will return.

The feelings we suffer during grief gradually disappear. However, during the first year, these feelings may get so severe that sometimes we may think we're going crazy.

During this time we may be susceptible to accidents, illness, forgetfulness, and constant crying. This is a normal part of the grieving process and you should expect these things to happen. Because this grieving period is important, experts urge us not to make *any major decisions* the first year after a loss.

## A TIME FOR ACCEPTANCE, A TIME TO TAKE CARE

When the full impact of death or divorce sets in, we begin to realize our lost mate will not return. Despair, depression, and guilt may make us act irrational and feel irritable. Grief continues until we gradually come to a time of acceptance. This takes time. If we don't put effort into the healing process, we may lengthen the grief and suffering, possibly causing permanent damage to ourselves.

Experts suggest that before making any changes in your lifestyle, take care to follow these simple tips during your period of grief:

*Get proper nutrition* whether you feel like it or not.
*Get some form of regular exercise.*
*Get around and associate* with people.
*Go back to work or do something useful* as soon as possible.
*Report physical complaints* to your doctor.
*Remember to be very careful.* Your emotions are suffering trauma, which makes your body vulnerable to accidents.
*During your time of mourning, avoid the temptation* to drink too much, smoke more than usual, or overuse tranquilizers and pain medications.

## IS ANY CHANGE A GOOD CHANGE?

When Francis, 53, left her abusive husband, a prominent doctor, she knew she faced a tremendous drop in income, but she had no options. She wanted to get as far
away from him as possible.

After the divorce, she and her 7-year-old daughter
traveled across the country to southern Florida, where she
worked in commercial real estate. Although she was used
to living in a spacious two-story home, she welcomed
moving into their tiny garden apartment, because it provided a safe place. "I felt like I was coming home," says
Francis, "and I welcomed a new peace of mind." In her
complex, she formed new single friends, who went to
movies with her or out to dinner. A friend in an apartment upstairs cared for her daughter if she worked late,
and her complex became a supportive community. Even
though her monetary lifestyle changed drastically, Francis
appreciated her new freedom as she began to rebuild her
life.

## TO SELL OR NOT TO SELL, THAT
## IS THE QUESTION

Did you know that deciding whether or not to keep or
sell your home may be one of the most emotional decisions you'll make? "But the hardest hit may not be in
your heart, but in your bank account," says Kerry Hannon, a financial adviser and author of *Suddenly Single—A
Money Guide*.

According to Ms. Hannon, hanging onto the house

may not be smart. If you're offered the house in the divorce settlement, take it, she says, but don't necessarily keep it. Keeping the house could be like a "ball and chain" around your ankle. In her Internet column for iVillage.com, Ms. Hannon describes one woman who discovered that she and her daughter were better off without the house.

During her marriage, this woman and her husband struggled to keep up the payments, even with two incomes. Selling gave her enough money to pay off most of the debt and get through the lease and moving expenses. After a death or divorce, says Ms. Hannon, who is also a reporter and columnist for *USA Today*, you may be tempted to hold onto your home. But are you aware of the actual costs of running a home, including insurance, repairs, maintenance, lawn care, and property taxes?

Many women are overwhelmed by the cost of home upkeep. Although they gain custody of the house and the children, they also gain custody of the debt. "If a woman is not in the workforce, or if she makes less than her husband did, she may be facing an unmanageable situation," says career transition consultant John McDorman.

Women from high-income marriages may face a more difficult battle, says Mr. McDorman. If they do not work, they may have no income coming in. Suddenly, they're falling from high on the social ladder to a lower rung.

How can you protect yourself? "Get rid of the expensive home and get realistic about [your] money situation," says Mr. McDorman, also an out-placement counselor for Fortune 500 companies.

And if you're divorcing, be aware that statistics show

that a woman's income drops by 45 percent after a divorce, while the man's rises 15 percent.

So what can you do about this?

Adriane G. Berg, a financial consultant, knows how women can radically improve their monetary situation and how they can move from nothing financially to a more comfortable status. "When my mother was 41 years old, my father died of a sudden stroke, leaving her penniless overnight. No savings, no insurance. And since she had never worked, no job. Plus, my aunt owned the home we lived in.

"Today, my mother is a beautiful 83-year-old woman who put me through college and law school, and still buys my 8-year-old daughter clothes."

What was her secret? Low-cost housing. Ms. Berg's mother moved from her dream home into a 600-square-foot apartment, furnishing it with "the best of her house." And what did she gain? "In reality, the best real estate is outpaced by the stock market. A house is not always the great investment you may think it is, but instead, it may be a luxury. If you can give it up, your financial life opens up . . . free from taxes, a mortgage, insurance, repairs, and more. Your budget sighs with relief."

That's why selling your house and investing the equity may be a smart choice, experts say.

## GETTING READY

If you're suddenly single, your pace is frantic. Paying the bills on time, getting to work on time, picking up the kids on time, and maybe even having some time for yourself. That's why making cool, calm decisions is not only difficult but laughable. So, where should you start?

Get together a "team" to walk you through this transition. Meet with them weekly. Ask their advice. Tell them your plans. And encourage them to hold you accountable for your actions by seeing that you follow through with your goals and live up to your expectations.

This team of people should be made up of an old friend, someone you currently know, and someone you don't know. Choose people who have successfully overcome adversity in their lives. They should not only guide but inspire you.

## IS YOUR EX PREVENTING YOU FROM MOVING?

According to a *Newsweek* article (February 2000), "The Moving-Van Wars," relocation is becoming a legal problem for ex-spouses.

In Missouri, it's illegal for a divorced parent to move over an ex's objection, preserving the rights of non-custodial parents.

Family-law experts report that with remarriage and a healthy economy, a more mobile work force has been created, causing more and more custodial parents to want to move. Consequently, the non-custodial parents are being left behind, and they are complaining to custody judges. "The trend has been toward balancing the burden of both parents," says Linda Elrod, editor of the American Bar Association's *Family Law Quarterly.* "The judge doesn't automatically rule that one parent can't move because the other doesn't want them to."

But what about the increase of mobility? The fact that

more and more women hold demanding jobs that require them to transfer to other areas increases the problem. Picking up and moving is not as easy as it sounds. In states like Illinois and Missouri, the parent who wishes to leave has to prove that relocation is in the interest of the child. In Jane Hicks's case, she is trapped in Missouri. After she remarried in 1997, she tried to move her two children to her new husband's residence in Illinois, just 95 miles away. But the Missouri judge ruled that her ex has a right to have continued access to his children. Hicks "feels like a hostage," she says. "The only thing I can do is try and get the law changed."

## JOB RELOCATION

If you're suddenly single, the last thing you want to think about is your career, but your job security is of utmost importance. More of this subject will be covered in the following chapter.

According to Mr. McDorman, who counsels hundreds of people a year on making career changes, there are a few ways to determine if you need to relocate:

- *Focus.* Work through your grief, so that you can focus on practical matters.
- *Emotional support.* Get a support system you can trust, i.e., relatives, siblings, or old friends. If there are children involved, should they be separated from their father?
- *Finances.* Investigate the marketplace in your geographic area to determine if there are enough

jobs. If you're in a small or rural area, you may have to move.

- *Jobs.* If you're offered a job in another locale, weigh salary, benefits, moving costs, and cost of living expenses. Don't be overly flattered. Be cautious!
- *Investigate.* Research job opportunities of a particular region, as well as moving costs, through such web sites as Places Rated Almanac and Allied Van Lines. Don't forget: There are more costs to moving than renting moving vans. So before you move make sure your furniture can fit into the new house or apartment. Also ask: How far will I have to commute? What about adequate schools, hospitals, shopping centers, and neighborhood safety?

## PUTTING YOUR HOUSE ON THE MARKET

In most cases, it's advisable to use a real estate agent or broker, which will cost around six percent of the selling price of the house.

In choosing a realtor, ask friends, neighbors, and colleagues for recommendations. Seek a reputable agent who specializes in your kind of property. Choose an agent who's a member of a multiple-listing service, which will give your home maximum exposure to the market. Don't forget to inquire how your house will be marketed or if the agent will hold an open house.

### Before Signing a Contract

- Make sure it's the standard three to six months.
- Interview several agents and check their references.
- Ask yourself: Do you feel comfortable with this agent? Is he or she accessible to you?
- Beware of any agent who suggests an unusually high selling price. He could be using this method to get you to sign with him, then he'll drop the price later.
- Don't overprice your house.
- Make a good first impression; see to it that your house has "drive-up appeal." Repair gutters and trim. Paint exterior. Trim bushes. Keep lawn mowed and trimmed. Plant flowers. Be sure the inside of your house is clean and uncluttered. Make sure the kitchen and bathroom sparkle.
- Be honest about defects. Don't deceive buyers.
- List utility costs. Have a list of the last 12 months' utility costs.

SOURCE: *After He's Gone: A Guide For Widowed and Divorced Women* by Barbara Tom Jowell and Donnette Schwisow (Carol Publishing Group, 1997)

## GO FOR IT!

Maureen, 63, is a risk-taker, and she's not afraid to admit it. At the age of 18, she graduated fifth in her class and was awarded a partial scholarship to a nearby college, but her parents were unable to come up with the additional money, so she could not attend school.

But this didn't stop her. After acing a Civil Service test, she boarded a train to Washington, D.C., where she began work for the U.S. Navy as a legal assistant.

Twenty-five years later, after the sudden death of her husband, she again set out on her own. "I wanted to get away from my home. There were memories of Bob in all the rooms," she says. "And I couldn't take it anymore. I just wanted to escape."

In a little over a year, she negotiated the sale of her home and moved to Maine.

After moving she landed a new job, beating out 65 other applicants. Then, she found a new joy. "I learned that being alone doesn't have to be lonely," she says. After purchasing a seaside cottage, she enjoyed long walks on the beach and planting peonies in her garden. She also enjoyed staying up until the wee hours to knit or sew, as well as eating when she felt like it. Or, in spite of her children's protests, she likes boarding a bus to a nearby casino and gambling until dawn.

"After more than 30 years of being a wife and mother, I thought it was my time," she explains. "I was ready. Relocating made me come alive."

## DID YOU KNOW?

Free pamphlets concerning moving may be found at your local post office or your chamber of commerce. Additional information can be obtained from your local telephone company.

## TIPS FOR MAKING HAPPY CAREER CHOICES

- What to do first: Gather a group of pros, mentors, and friends to meet with you weekly for advice and direction. Make sure they hold you accountable for your actions by seeing that you follow through with your goals.
- Offered a job? Don't accept a job relocation too hastily. Take your time and consider schools, property values, location of nearby stores, crime safety, resale value of your home, etc.
- Does your salary match moving needs, home purchase costs?
- Consider the emotional impact the move will have on your kids. Will they miss their dad? Is he present in their lives?

**IS RELOCATING FOR YOU?**

- Are you ready to leave your home? Are you ready to leave your old neighborhood? Your friends? Your butcher, baker, pastor, rabbi?
- What will you do when you relocate? Will you be able to drive? Will your new neighborhood be safe?
- If you have children, is the school safe? Is it rated high academically? How will your children adjust?

## CHAPTER 4 REVIEW: RELOCATING IS A MOVING EXPERIENCE, BUT YOU COULD BE HAPPIER STAYING PUT

- **Do nothing the first year** after a death or divorce. Get proper nutrition, exercise, associate with people, go back to work, avoid excessive alcohol and smoking.
- **Make sure you are moving for the right reasons.** Moving just to change is not enough. Consider all that you'll be leaving behind, like friends, acquaintances, your church, your weekly bingo game, people you can trust and depend on. Your memories.
- **Can you afford to move?** Can you afford *not* to? Make sure you investigate this closely. Many single women have a tough time hanging onto their house with only one paycheck. Remember,

selling a home and liquidating the capital can free you up.

- **After you've made a complete inventory,** then you can consider a change.
- **Remember,** women over 60 have a harder time moving. Remaining near what's familiar to you may prove more beneficial.

## Chapter Five

# starting from scratch

Gingerly sitting on a pillow, the petite, five-foot-one woman maneuvered the pickup truck down the bumpy country road on her way to the city. With her 10-year-old son by her side, Carrie drove into the night, Garth Brooks blasting from the radio. Although hesitant to leave her hometown, she knew this was the right decision. After two failed marriages, no child support, and no college degree, Carrie, 36, had few career options.

All she had was hope.

So when a friend from Little Rock, Arkansas, offered her a place in her beauty salon, Carrie knew this was her chance. Although hesitant to leave her home town, she was eager to start over, even if it meant starting from scratch.

"Once I made up my mind, I never looked back," she says. "I had no choice. I had to succeed. If not for me, then for my child." After attending beauty school, she became a licensed manicurist, leasing a space in her friend's beauty salon. Starting with no salary, Carrie slowly but surely built her client base, earning $50 in commissions a day, and then $200 a day.

It wasn't always easy. Because her work was seasonal, she subsidized her earnings by catering parties, tending bar, and cleaning houses. One Christmas, she took a part-time job at a jewelry store overlooking an ice rink where her son skated while she worked.

Asked about being self-employed, she replies, "I love being my own boss. Giving manicures to others nurtures me, as I've discovered the power of touch."

Having a more flexible schedule, Carrie is able to get home early or be available to take her son to soccer games. In the middle of manicuring a client's nails, Carrie frequently takes calls from her son, discussing his home-work or outside school activities.

"John, that's great. I'm so proud of you!" she says when he announces being accepted in the talented-and-gifted program. Like most working moms, Carrie is jug-gling as fast as she can. But she does it well, and her clients not only understand, they admire her.

"I always knew I could make it," she says.

At the age of 15, she left home, fleeing from an alco-holic mother. Although she later moved in with an aunt, Carrie felt like she was on her own at a young age. "My life hasn't been easy but it has made me tough. I know how to survive."

**Helen, after 11 years of marriage.** Helen arrived in Phoenix, Arizona with two children in tow, ages 9 and 14, and a wasted marriage in the trash can. Resembling the out-of-work single mom in the movie *Erin Brockovich* starring Julia Roberts, she didn't take no for an answer. After being out of the work force for five years, she didn't have time to polish her job skills. "I had two months before the money ran out," she says, "and I needed to find the right job quickly."

With help from her church, Helen set up an interview with a local non-profit agency for a job as communications director. "With a background in accounting, I didn't have the specific skills they required, but I knew I'd be good at the job. I was organized, people-smart, and a good public speaker."

"I told them I had two offers on the table, and I needed to know something by the end of the week," she says, laughing. Where did she get such a gutsy approach?

Like Erin Brockovich, "I was desperate," Helen admits, "but the job was perfect for me. It had flexible hours and it was a few minutes' drive from my children's school." For Helen, getting a job was easy, compared to the life she'd been living.

## BUT WHAT IF YOU'VE LED A MORE SHELTERED LIFE?

Are you prepared for living alone? *With one out of two marriages ending in divorce, and women typically outliving their spouses by 7 to 12 years, many of us are destined to live alone at some time in our lives.*

After a loss, you are faced with difficult decisions concerning your own and your children's welfare. Who will put them through college? Should you return to work? What type of job should you get? How qualified are you?

## THE WINDING ROAD FOR WIDOWS

After the funeral guests leave, reality sets in. At 58, Martha discovered her financial situation was not nearly as stable as she had imagined. So, with two children in college, she rented out rooms in her spacious home and took a clerical job as well.

Like Martha, some people may need a job to support their family and get better health insurance. Widows must take charge of their finances from the get-go! It's easy to go into denial. To push the bills into a drawer. But things will only get worse if you don't deal with them immediately.

**Amanda: no husband and the money going fast.** When her husband became seriously ill, Amanda's son moved in to care for him. Two years later, her husband died, and Amanda had to learn to live without him. At first, she was fearful of running through her money. She met with a financial adviser and created a workable budget. She cut down on entertainment expenses, gas, and utilities. Now, she's considering asking her son to move out. "I don't need him any longer. He runs up unnecessary expenses with food and utilities," she says. "Although I appreciate what he's done, I no longer need to be taken care of. I value my privacy."

## ENTERING THE JOB MARKET

After 21 years of marriage, Sara started over.

At 42, she finished college. A year later, she got her

master's degree in social work. During that time, she sold her posh estate in Atlanta and moved into a tiny apartment overlooking a parking lot.

In order to pay her college expenses, Sara lived very frugally, taking a bus to and from school in order to save on gas. "In two years, I went to only two movies," says Sara. "I didn't do anything but study and go to school."

Sara went on to become a mental health counselor for the psychiatric department of a leading hospital. But her road to financial independence was difficult.

"I learned that a lack of money puts you in a position of helplessness, vulnerability, and dependency," Sara says. "I regret all the years in my marriage that I wasted doing nothing. I was so busy running the garden club and volunteering that when I divorced, I had to start over. I didn't even have a college degree."

**Sue at 52.** "It was my fantasy that I'd be happily married forever." Sue was married to a CEO of a large company. When she learned of her husband's affairs, it was too late to make amends. "It was difficult to turn the other way when he started showing up in public with other women. I think it was his way of hurting me."

Like many women, Sue started dating her husband in high school. She married when she was 22 and devoted her time to her children and attending company functions with her husband. During the divorce, she was incapable of fighting. "I just wanted to get it over with," she says, and ultimately, her husband hid the assets, leaving her with very little.

When Sue speaks of her husband, her voice is laced

with sarcasm. "I thought I'd be a good little girl, and he'd take care of me." After the divorce, she had to start from scratch to rebuild her life.

Determined to put the divorce behind her, she got a business degree and now works as a financial planner. After recently purchasing her own home, she's proud of her financial gains. "If I'd only started sooner," she says. "I would've valued my independence more, realizing that a marriage needs to be a equal partnership."

## COURAGE TO GO ON

Like many women who are suddenly single, you may find your life turned inside-out. You're not only grieving, but you're in a panic about becoming the breadwinner. Besides having to raise your children, you've inherited the burden of paying for a mortgage, food, utilities, gas for the car, entertainment, and more. And you have to do it all alone.

What if you've spent your life putting others first? How do you develop the courage to go on? And how do you plan for your future?

According to therapist Virginia Clemente, "Women need to quit living in a fairy tale. Everyone wants to be taken care of, but that's not realistic."

## PREPARING TO LIVE ALONE: CREATE A PLAN OF ACTION . . . NOW

With the high divorce rate and the average age of widowhood at 56, it's never too early to prepare to live alone.

"If your husband leaves you, don't waste time hoping he'll return," Ms. Clemente says. "That rarely happens."

Instead, she advises using the time while you're married or separated to develop a survival plan.

- Collect information. Find out where the money is. Determine how much is coming in and how much is going out. How much will it take to live?
- Get credit cards in your own name.
- Go back to school.
- Assess and update your marketable skills.

Experts recommend that you *never leave a marriage unprepared*. If you're a displaced homemaker, you've lost your lifetime job. "There's no difference in being severed from your job as a CEO of the house versus CEO of a company," says John McDorman, career transition counselor. If you're trying to enter the job market and you're negotiating a divorce, ask the attorney to include these items in the divorce decree:

- Severance pay while you're looking for a job.
- Out-placement counseling fee of at least $15,000. You'll need this amount to find a good job.
- Benefits continuation—that is, health benefits until you find a job.
- Is your husband self-employed? Then demand seed capital in your husband's business. After all, you helped him build the business by managing his household and children while he worked.

## HOW MUCH TIME DO I HAVE
## TO FIND A JOB?

Are you pressed for cash? After a divorce or death, you're in a such a rush to settle your finances that you often take a lesser job. In his book, *What Color Is Your Parachute?* (Ten Speed Press, 1995), Richard Nelson Bolles urges job seekers to determine how much time they have before they absolutely need to find a job. The average length of a job hunt lasts for 18.4 weeks (about 4.5 months), says Mr. Bolles, and it's not at all unusual to take nine months to find a job. So how are you going to survive for months with no work?

## CONSIDER USING YOUR SAVINGS OR
## BORROWED INCOME

If you're divorcing, request funds in the divorce decree to cover your expenses while job hunting. If you're a widow, use your husband's social security (which you should apply for immediately upon his death). Now, total up your income, cut costs where you can, then compare your income to your monthly expenses. "The earlier you get started, the more lead time you give yourself," says Mr. Bolles.

There's more. The best way to determine how much money you need to survive on as a single woman is to take an inventory of your own finances. Act like a detective, inquiring about your personal bank accounts, investments, taxes, stocks, or bonds (explained more in Chapter 9). Remember, *knowledge is power!*

Many women tend to hand over power to their husbands in marriage. "In my practice, I find that the person who is primarily earning the most money tends to be more empowered," says Leotta Alexander, a family law attorney. "I'm still amazed at how many women have no clue about their finances. Some don't know how much money their husbands make. They take the money he gives them and pay household expenses with it. But they don't know the details about their finances or investments." This leaves women in the dark when it comes to uncovering their resources. It prevents them from realistically evaluating how much time they have before they need to get a job, as well as other issues.

When women knowingly hand over power to their mates, continues Ms. Alexander, they begin to let go of making their own decisions. And, after a divorce, they're more passive. They focus on trying to get their husband back. They want to be fair. They don't want to hurt him. They depend on him.

"I ask them: What's he done to be fair to *you?*" says Ms. Alexander. "You need to get angry. You need to get past this. This guy is hurting you. You don't need to sit there like a patsy and take it."

However, she points out that many women don't listen. They're concentrating on the fact that they've lost their relationship, instead of concentrating on the financial part.

This prevents them from moving on. It prevents them from looking closely at their finances to determine what they need to do. It prevents them from making financial demands in the divorce, and finally, it prevents them from looking for a job.

In the end, many women are in emotional turmoil, and they haven't thought out what can they do to support themselves or how can they get a career on track.

## OKAY, YOUR LOSS IS ALMOST FINALIZED

If it's a divorce, the mess is almost over with. If a death has occurred, the funeral bills are paid. You've received your husband's life insurance—it may not be the amount you thought, but it's a beginning.

At last your head is clear. And you know you need to start the job search. See the sidebar on the next page to learn ways to assess your skills.

## HOW TO POSITION YOURSELF IN THE MARKETPLACE

Before you can sell yourself to others, you need to recognize your *marketable skills*. And don't overlook your volunteer work. Ask yourself: Have you raised over $10,000 at your school auction? Are you producing a homeowners' newsletter? Do you know word processing or computer graphics? Can you do public speaking? Substitute teaching? Think, think, think!

All of these are marketable skills. And, what is more, they are *transferable* skills, says Taunee Besson, a career columnist for Oxygen.com. The key to assessing your skills is recognizing what you enjoy doing, and how it will also support you financially. Volunteer work is a perfect match for work in the non-profit sector. "I've seen full-time volunteers build credentials, enabling them to move

## HOW TO TURN YOUR SKILLS INTO A CAREER

- What are your marketable skills? Which of these skills do you enjoy?
- Where do you want to use these skills?
- Which organizations use people with your skills?
- Are they reputable organizations? Do you share the same goals?
- If these organizations don't use people with your skills, could you persuade them to?
- What are the names of the organizations? Are they located in areas or cities you'd consider living in?
- What are the problems or challenges of these organizations, particularly in the departments or areas where you might be working?
- As you approach various departments, find out who makes the final decision in hiring. (Avoid the personnel department unless you're looking for an entry-level job.)

SOURCE: *What Color Is Your Parachute?* by Richard Nelson Bolles (Ten Speed Press, 1995)

easily into the non-profit sector with a demanding position," Ms. Besson says.

Marriage and family therapist Virginia Clemente agrees. She advises women in transition to give themselves a lot of credit for all they've done. "In a marriage, we've been both nurturers and guides. We've encouraged our husbands in their climb to success. We've cared for ailing parents. We've managed family finances, organized and prepared nutritious meals, or counseled doctors and teachers," says Ms. Clemente, a 10-year leader of singles workshops for the United Methodist Church.

Just because you didn't get paid for these accomplishments, don't underrate them or totally discount them.

## GET READY TO SELL YOURSELF

After you discover what you can do, start talking to others, using all your connections. Gather information about job opportunities by networking. Call family members, friends, or friends of friends, telling them you're looking for a job. If you belong to a church or temple, perhaps other members can refer you to an employer. At your church, have you done a good job heading a committee or teaching Sunday school? Can someone there vouch for your character? Before interviewing for a job, use all your connections and do your homework. Don't just rely on the classified ads.

## THE INFORMATIONAL INTERVIEW

If you're working up the nerve to interview, you're probably asking yourself: "What do I say? How do I sell myself? Should I research the company? And how do I do that?" According to Taunee Besson, author of *National Business Employment Weekly Resumes* (Wiley & Sons, 1994), an *informational interview* can help you by identifying potential employers and uncovering positions not filled through executive search firms. These interviews also allow you to ask the employer all about her company, so you can see if your skills match her needs.

**Beth's story.** Beth took pride in being an "earth mother." She nursed her children until they were toddlers. Later she would select fresh vegetables at the farmer's market, return home, and cook and puree them into baby food. On top of that, every year she threw a neighborhood Christmas party where friendly "elves" led the children in frosting cookies, stringing popcorn, and singing Christmas carols.

Leaving the safety of her domestic life was difficult for Beth. She was fearful of returning to work after a 9-year absence. In fact, she was scared to death. "Each year I stayed at home with my children, I lost confidence in my ability to work outside the home," she says.

"I had no skills, but I was tenacious," she adds. A closet poet, Beth had a rusty English degree. While taking a health-care course at community college, she designed a term project where she surveyed various hospital communication departments within the city.

When she was ready to interview, she used that research to provide good job leads. She was on her way. One interview led to another, until finally she landed a job in public relations with a large metropolitan hospital.

What does she say about her success? "I wasn't sure I could do it," Beth says. "But I didn't give up ... it just took time."

### How Do You Schedule an Informational Interview?

Get a reference from a friend. Many times an employer may talk to you as a favor to her friend. Employers tend to agree to informational interviews because "they like to be experts—turning to them for advice flatters them," as Ms. Besson says. People like to talk about themselves, basking in a listener's undivided attention. After all, how many of us have an opportunity to play "expert" before an appreciative audience?

On the flip side, meeting with you on an information basis offers a low-risk way to evaluate your potential. "Interviewing employees is hard work and time-consuming," Ms. Besson says. "In an informational interview, you do all the work, you research the company, prepare the questions and take the interviewing lead."

**DID YOU KNOW?**

- An informational interview is far less stressful because candidates seek information, not actual jobs.
- The interviewer is you, the person who is trying to learn more about the job market. The interviewee is the company representative.
- Job hunters take the initiative in making the appointment, not the employers.
- Did you know you can impress a potential employer with your enthusiasm? If they have an opening in the future, they'll be sure to remember you!

**WHAT DO YOU SAY IN AN INFORMATIONAL INTERVIEW?**

- Tell me about your company. How did it get started?
- Describe its growth.
- Can you describe its sales volume, annual budget, and number of employees?
- What about its profit, offices, stores, or corporate headquarters?
- What are the company's major products and services, experience, major areas of concentration, and new developments?
- Is it community-spirited and does it profess an interest in cultivating its employees?
- What kinds of careers does it offer?
- Which of my specific experiences, personality traits, or skills might interest this company?

SOURCE: *National Business Employment Weekly Resumes* by Taunee Besson

## TEMPORARY WORK

Did you know that temporary employment agencies can provide great training for women just entering or returning to the work force? You can choose the days and hours you want to work and the assignments you want to take.

Currently, temp agencies report that they employ many mothers returning to work after a long absence, as well as women seeking to begin or change careers.

David Schlecker, an employment manager, agrees. "In my opinion, temping is the way to go if you've been out of the work force, and for whatever reason, you're coming back after a long absence."

## RETIREES WELCOME TOO

Are you worried about age discrimination? If you're a new widow, you may need to return to work, and if you want to work on a temporary basis, then temping is for you. Employers have increased interest in hiring older women, career experts say, because they generally have a lot of work experience and are very reliable.

And retirees have the best of both worlds, greater job flexibility and guaranteed income. Some even qualify for benefits. Take Ann Rash, an executive secretary, who works three days a week, allowing her to pursue her one great passion: travel.

## THE POWER OF RE-PACKAGING

If you're thinking about returning to school to get a graduate degree or an MBA, think again. Instead of vesting another year or two in more education, why not try to repackage yourself?

"Many women think they need to retrain [when re-entering the work force], when all they need to do is repackage their existing skills," says John McDorman, an out-placement counselor for Fortune 500 companies.

Think of the skills you have, he suggests, and try to find a new use for them. Make a list of volunteer services such as public speaking, heading committees, or organizing fund raisers, and see how they'd fit into educational or counseling jobs.

## DON'T BE SHY

A lot of women fail to mention volunteer work because they don't value it. They think it has to be done in a "real" office to count as work. What women returning to the work force should have are these attributes: confidence, competence, and contacts.

Once you're ready for the job force, call everyone you know and tell them what kind of job you're looking for.

Then, set up informational interviews with qualified people hiring in the field you've chosen. Maybe you won't get a job that day, but three months later, when a position opens, that manager may remember you (and your nice thank-you note) and pull out your resume.

Whatever you do, *don't rely on classified ads*. Only 15 to 20 percent of all jobs are found that way. Instead, try joining women's organizations like the YWCA, Women in Communications, the International Association of Business Communicators, the Association of Business Professionals, or your local chamber of commerce. And keep networking, because often it's not *what* you know but *who* you know that leads to a job.

Don't expect to find a job quickly. The right job will most likely take you longer to find.

## TWO-MINUTE COMMERCIAL

In the meantime, says Ms. Besson, make up a two-minute "commercial" about yourself describing the job you can do and why you'd be good at it. Then, update your skills.

## WHAT TO DO ABOUT YOUR RESUME

Are you returning to the same career? You may be surprised at some of the changes that have taken place since your absence. If you've used your time wisely, you've kept up with changes in your field. If not, it may be time for some cramming. To bone up on what's been going on, read industry news and start talking to people in your field.

Got a gap in your resume? Try using a *functional resume* instead of a *chronological* one. The functional resume highlights your skills. The chronological one focuses on each job you've held.

### Resume-Writing Tips

Writing your first resume can be a daunting experience.

Following is a list of tips compiled from the advice of employers, career counselors, and recent graduates whose resumes helped them land meaningful employment.

- Pay careful attention to spelling, punctuation, grammar, and style.

**DID YOU KNOW?**

It's crucial to make a *positive statement* about your
absence from the job force. Explain that you took
time off to raise a family, and don't apologize!

* Proofread carefully, using a dictionary and style
  book, and have several other people proofread as
  well.
* Organize information in a logical fashion.
* Keep descriptions clear and to the point.
* Use a simple, easy-to-read font such as Times,
  Palatino, Helvetica, or Arial.
* Confine your information to one page.
* Include as much work experience as possible,
  even if it doesn't relate obviously to the job
  you're seeking.
* Tailor your information to the job you're seeking.
* Seek help at your career services center or local
  library.

### Brag on Yourself

Many of us are caught up in why we're *not* marketable, and we may not be aware of the fact that we all
have transferable skills such as knowledge, adaptability,
attitude, character, and "teamsmanship," regardless of
specific working skills.

"When employers are looking at hiring someone," says Ms. Besson, "they're considering if you *can* do the job, if you *will* do the job, and if you *want* the job. Often people get hired who may not have the same level of expertise [as other job candidates], but they show an interest in the company and a good attitude. They show they're in a learning mode."

What about women who have stayed home with their children? "Mothers looking for work" all have strong working skills, says Ms. Besson. "They persevere, they nurture, they create a team. Many have lots of traits employers would love to have."

## RETURNING TO SCHOOL

Did you know that community colleges offer intense counseling and courses for those re-entering the work force?

If you're trying to regenerate your credentials, help may be just around the corner.

### *Making the Grade*

When Susie Smoot-Brown returned to college at 47, she was overwhelmed by fear. She worried about competing with younger students, about passing math, about writing a composition. She was even afraid to look her professor in the eye.

As mentioned in Chapter 1, she knew other women felt the same way, so she did something about it.

While working part-time at her college counseling office, she created a support group, "Women of Wisdom," for older female students (ages 25 to 65) who shared the same mission: to complete their college degrees with courage and confidence.

Now, four years later, WOW offers comfort to women returning to school after long absences.

### Who's Going Back to School?

In 1998, according to the Department of Commerce, women comprised 59.8 percent of the work force. More and more women are enrolling in college to better themselves, but regardless of their educational status, the road back is still rocky.

"Many women returning to school walk the same path," says Ms. Smoot-Brown, now an adjunct college professor. "They are anxious about how they can compete on tests. And they worry about their rusty study skills."

### Fear Not

Karen Belgard, 55, agrees. She is a student and a member of WOW. After being laid off from her secretarial job three years ago, she entered college for the first time. "I was at such a low point. I was afraid to take a course for credit."

But she never gave up. She took one accredited class, then a few more. Her confidence grew as she learned to outline chapters and to e-mail her professors when she didn't understand a subject. "That way I avoided confronting them," says Ms. Belgard, who is completing a degree in computer information systems.

"Even the summer sessions are fast and furious," she adds. "But if I take just one course, I can make it. It goes by quickly in five weeks."

Roxanne Underwood, another WOW member, also

struggles with returning to school. "I'm a slow reader, and I have to go over and over the material to get it," she says.

Ms. Underwood is unable to answer the teacher when called upon. "I get a terrible feeling in the pit of my stomach when I can't verbalize my thoughts, and I'm worried about it."

"I don't think you can drop a screen and say, 'That's the end of that feeling,'" Ms. Smoot-Brown encouragingly tells the group. "Progress is one step at a time, a journey, and I see changes in you each week."

### *You Can Do It*

Susan Hawthorne, a psychotherapist who counsels college and graduate students, believes that women returning to college are often afraid they won't be bright enough, or they won't remember how to study.

Many women try to hide the fact that they don't have a college degree, she says, because so much of their self-esteem is tied to it.

She has found, however, that women returning to school make the best students, because they draw on life experiences and it's their choice to attend school. "I've found that women returning to school are more adept at handling time management, and they are rewarded in a school setting. That's why they study more—the payoff is high."

In the end, continues Ms. Hawthorne, the school setting richly rewards female students, because "when women receive a degree, they realize how capable they are and how much they have to offer."

## CHAPTER 5 REVIEW: GET A JOB

- **Identify your skills.** This is one of the biggest problems for women. Most women returning to the work force feel like they don't have any skills.
- **Homemaking *is* a job.** Homemakers should realize they've had to learn valuable, everyday job skills around the house, such as organizing, planning, budgeting, managing, supervising, and teaching.
- **Use a "functional resume."** This is a particularly wise move for women who've been out of the job market for some time because it highlights skills and abilities, rather than specific jobs or chronological experience.
- **Volunteer.** It's an excellent way to gain new skills, if you can afford to donate your time.
- **Network.** It's the best way to find a job. If you rely solely on the newspaper, you'll be competing with hundreds of other people.
- **Announce your availability.** Start by telling everyone you know and meet that you're looking for work. Call companies to ask about openings or schedule an appointment with the human resources office.
- **Visit companies personally.** Yes, just walk in. "It is difficult," says Kathy Froede, director of the YWCA Women in Transition Program, "but what's the worst thing that will happen? You can get thrown out of the office. But that never really happens."

- **Update yourself.** Update your computer skills. This is vital to enhancing employment capabilities. If you had a career before leaving work, update yourself on current trends by contacting colleagues and reading professional journals.

## Chapter Six

# your money matters

Betty Berkeley, a retirement planning consultant, says married women are often the least prepared financially. "They often don't concern themselves with their financial future, because they think they will be taken care of the rest of their lives," says Ms. Berkeley, an AARP spokesperson. "This is a big mistake because in three out of four marriages, the woman is the survivor."

Whether we are spendthrifts or savers, money governs our lives. Then why do women often avoid money matters? Why do we tend to pass the responsibility to another individual . . . whether it's our husband, lover, or father? Are we afraid of math? Are we hoping that someone will rescue us from facing reality?

When we avoid thinking about or planning for tomorrow, we are not protecting ourselves or our loved ones. We are denying our future ability to survive financially.

Many women are guilty of this tendency. Historically, they tend to leave finances to their spouse, and this can lead to a very serious financial situation.

Even those with high-powered jobs are guilty of neglecting daily money matters. It's easy to let someone else tend to finances.

Marilyn Steele of Fountain Valley, California, was 40 years old when she was overcome by the fear that she might very well end up "growing old . . . poor." Ms. Steele, a teacher, had been through two failed marriages and had a teenage son to raise before it occurred to her that she had not been putting money away for retirement.

After meeting with a financial planner, she thought: "If I am going to take care of my son, I've got to take care of myself first." She now puts $300 a month into a tax-sheltered account. "If it's money you never see, you can learn to live without it," she says.

## WHAT ABOUT YOU?

If you're college educated and gainfully employed, you may think you're financially savvy and secure. But you may be wrong. Very wrong.

The inability to manage assets effectively is a failing of millions of women, including those who are competent, knowledgeable, and skilled. Women like you and me.

What if you are in the middle of a divorce? Or newly widowed? How will you find the time to become a skilled money manager? When you're in the throes of grieving, how will you be able to think about finances?

*You must take the time, before time catches up with you.*

The National Center for Women and Retirement Research at New York's Long Island University reports that many women are often one paycheck away from poverty and that they are financially uneducated.

Financial experts say that it's important for women to learn how to hold onto their money and put it to work, because women can expect to spend a good percentage of their lives as independent single people.

They suggest the following ways to invest your money:

STOCKS. Recognizing the growing market for women investors, top brokerage houses are beginning to recruit women stock brokers to specifically solicit business from women. Did you know that with marketable stock to use as collateral, a woman today should have no trouble securing a bank loan?

MONEY MARKET INVESTMENTS. At the beginning of 2000, yields on Treasury Bills and money market Certificate of Deposits (CDs) are on the rise again. If you are a new investor, you'll be relieved to know that there is minimum risk in these areas. CDs are F.D.I.C.-insured deposits, while Treasury Bills are obligations of the U.S. Government. There's usually a nominal fee to buy T-bills or other government securities through a bank. Purchases of Treasury Bills can also be made directly through the Federal Reserve Bank at no additional cost.

MUTUAL FUNDS. Mutual funds are professionally managed pooled funds invested in a diverse portfolio of stocks. This gives the smaller investor a chance for diversification normally available only to a very large investor. Mutual funds also relieve you of the time and energy necessary to keep up with the individual stocks. Some funds have better performance records than others, and this should be considered when choosing where to invest. Money Market mutual funds allow smaller investors the opportunity to get higher yields by pooling their monies for purchase of large, higher-interest-paying money market securities. These are popular because of their rates and the advantage of liquidity.

SAVINGS. Are you building an estate? As a working woman, you may provide essentials for your family, like food, clothing, and shelter. But, as a single mother, you need to do more. In spite of your obligations, don't forget to save. Experts suggest paying yourself first, before anyone else. To investigate savings plans at your bank, ask to meet a bank officer and get to know her. Ask if someone is available to counsel you about investments. Then read, read, read. Read *Money*, the *Wall Street Journal*, and the business section of your local newspaper. Read financial and economic sections of business and news magazines. Read articles on personal finance in women's magazines.

There's a wealth of information in the library and at the book store, too. It's important to read, digest, and ask questions—and remember: It's your money, and no one is going to take care of it like you. If you haven't already begun, now is the time to assume responsibility for your own financial security.

## MIDDLE-AGED WOMEN

When Patti Longo's husband retired from the Navy in 1975, she took it upon herself to improve her financial education. "If I outlive him, I don't want to be left wondering," she says. Ms. Longo believes middle-aged and elderly women are most in need of financial help. As spokesperson for the Women's Financial Information Program, sponsored by the American Association of Retired Persons (AARP), Ms. Longo says: "Traditionally, women over 55 are left behind when it comes to financial matters. They were socialized to marry—and to believe their husband when he said, 'I'll take care of it.'" Because of this, she adds, women "are not prepared when it comes to death, divorce, disability or desertion."

## HOW TO GET STARTED

Jeffrey Becker, a certified financial planner in Los Angeles who conducts seminars on "Women and Investing," says the sooner women prepare, the better. "It's never too early for women to get their finances back in order." To get started, he suggests, go to the library and check out books on money management. This way, you can ask intelligent questions when meeting with a professional. Don't forget to inquire about such areas as budgeting, goal setting, buying insurance, caregiving expense, and how to file or locate important documents.

## WIDOWS IN JEOPARDY

The group of women at greatest risk of financial ruin are widows. "The average age of widowhood is now 56," Mr. Becker says. A Long Island University study reported that "Eighty percent of women are left in financial jeopardy through widowhood. And many of these women were not poor before the death of their husbands."

**Marjorie of Fountain Hills, Arizona, a case in point.** Marjorie was married for 36 years when her husband, Ed, died after a brief illness. After his death, the state of their finances was a shock to the widow. "When you are dealing with death, you don't know where to begin," says Marjorie. "You see the rope but you can't find the threads to grasp . . ."

After counseling with Howard Marchbanks, a district manager of Waddell and Reed Financial Services in Fullerton, Arizona, Marjorie was put on a strict budget.

"Women who live longer than their spouse," Marchbanks says, "may have to stretch fewer dollars farther." His suggestion is that they try to set aside three to six months' income in an emergency fund. Or to put away at least $100 a month.

If neither option is possible, consider trading in your high-interest credit card for one with lower interest. Then use the card only for emergencies. Mr. Marchbanks also warned women newly divorced to avoid salesmen trying to push them into making immediate financial decisions. "Wait a year, or longer," he says, "until you are less vulnerable."

## SIX "FIRST STEPS" WIDOWS SHOULD FOLLOW

Losing a loved one is painful. When you get over the shock, you're hit with guilt, anger, longing, and sadness—wrenching emotions that hit at the most unexpected times. When you're going through a loss, the last thing you may want to do is handle finances. Unfortunately, you need to deal with them as soon as possible. Kerry

Hannon, money expert columnist on iVillage.com, lists six steps to get you going:

**STEP 1: SLOW DOWN.** Suddenly, you're getting money in a lump sum from your husband's insurance or pension. But don't do anything with it. Wait at least six months before making a decision. Financial planners, relatives, or friends may be knocking on your door, promising you a "hot deal," but slow down. Deposit your money in a money market fund, Treasury bills, or short-term certificates of deposit (CDs).

**STEP 2: AVOID HOT TIPS.** Are you receiving calls from someone promising to be a financial whiz, offering you a "hot tip"? Did you know that crafty financial consultants prey on new widows? Step back and take this time to learn all about finances, so that later on, you'll make an educated decision.

**STEP 3: DETAILS, DETAILS.** Are you barraged with endless paperwork? Having trouble finding your joint tax returns, insurance policies, wills, brokerage and bank account statements, or your retirement account records? Take the time to get organized. It's your money and no one is going to take care of it like you.

**STEP 4: FIND A PLACE TO WORK.** You may have to use your card table or dining room table. Or spread papers out on a bookshelf. Then, try to work on these documents each day.

STEP 5: COPY DEATH CERTIFICATE. Send a copy of your husband's death certificate to your bank manager, your stockbroker, credit-card companies, insurers, employer, the Social Security Administration, and your state's office for inheritance tax.

STEP 6: PAY BILLS. In the midst of dealing with a funeral and your grief, many of us are tempted to ignore our bills. Don't! Procrastination will lead to disaster.

**DID YOU KNOW?**

Whether you're living alone or raising children, here's the latest on the current law regarding Social Security. Depending on your age, a widow receives the higher of two amounts: Benefits earned from her own work history or up to 100 percent of her husband's benefits. A widow can draw benefits as long as her children are under 18 (although these benefits phase out if she earns more than a certain amount). Children under 18 (19, if they're still in school) can draw benefits too.

## FINDING A FINANCIAL ADVISER

In their book *After He's Gone: A Guide for Widowed and Divorced Women* (Carol Publishing Group, 1997), Barbara Tom Jowell and Donnette Schwisow describe how important it is to plan for your future over an *extended lifetime*. Although you may receive life insurance or a pension in one lump sum, that amount must last you the *rest of your life*. Whether you are going through a divorce or death, your world has been turned upside-down, and this is the time to seek professional help.

But how do you know if someone is legitimate? Here are some quick tips: Look for a financial adviser who specializes in retirement accounts. Check his credentials. Are they licensed? Does he charge by the hour, or by taking a percentage of the return on investment? The latter may affect his judgment.

### CHOOSING A FINANCIAL PLANNING PROFESSIONAL

The National Center on Women and Aging at Brandeis University, Waltham, Massachusetts, advises that before choosing a financial advisor you ask a lot of questions. Select someone whom friends or associates have recommended. Ask about their qualifications, their investment philosophy, and how they are paid for their services.

**KEY QUESTIONS TO ASK**

- What is your professional training? What licenses, certifications, and registrations do you have? What credentials do you have to practice financial planning?
- Are you registered with the Federal Securities and Exchange Commission (SEC) or with a state agency?
- How do you keep up to date with developments in your field?
- Do you belong to any professional organizations?
- Are your clients in an income bracket similar to mine?
- Will you provide me with references?
- What is your attitude toward risk? How will you incorporate my particular situation into the financial planning process?
- How do you prepare a plan for your clients? How extensive is it?
- Do you keep in touch with your clients and make recommendations as appropriate? How often will we meet or talk?
- How are you compensated for various services?

## THE CHILD CARE CRUNCH

If you're a single mom, you're faced with finding quality daycare that's affordable. Here's the latest in child care costs:

**Daycare.** The Children's Defense Fund reports costs ranging from $4,210 per year in Dallas or $6,030 in Minneapolis to $8,800 in Boston.

**Nannies.** Will cost from $1,500 to $4,500 for 20 working days a month, plus room and board.

**Au Pair.** Will cost $125 per week, plus $500 a year toward tuition costs and another $4,400 or so to participate in the program, which includes the cost of airfare.

**Babysitting.** Charges for a typical preschool child start at $5 an hour.

## YOU DESERVE A TAX BREAK

Did you know the Child Tax Credit provides for a $500 tax credit in 2000 for each dependent child under age 17? Working parents are also offered tax breaks:

**Child care credit.** Do you pay someone to care for your child while you work? Then call 1-800-TAXFORM and request Child and Dependent Care Publication 503. Or download the form from the Internal Revenue Service's web site at http://www.irs.gov. Ann Douglas, author of *The Unofficial Guide to Childcare* (IDG Books, 1998), also has a web site: www.childcare-guide.com.

**Check it out with your company's HR department.** Your company's human resources department may offer a flexible spending account to help pay for your child care. This allows you to set aside pretax dollars for child care costs, which reduces your taxable income.

## SCARY STATISTICS

**Divorce and annulment.** As reported by the U.S. Census Bureau: "The average marriage in the United States lasts only seven years."

**The poverty rate.** Eighty percent of all widows who are living in poverty were not poor before the death of their husbands.

**On average,** women earn only 76 cents for every dollar that men earn, resulting in lower Social Security and pension benefits.

**In addition,** women spend more time outside the workforce (11.5 years for women versus 16 months for men), resulting in lower pension benefits. Also, women outnumber men in part-time jobs two to one. Part-timers are less likely to work for firms with retirement plans.

Phyllis Mutschler, executive director for the National Center on Women and Aging, says the longer a woman lives, the greater the probability she'll outlive her assets. "Women earn less, live longer, and have less savings," she says. More and more women are living longer than expected, and their pensions aren't indexed for inflation. If you live 15 or 25 years past retirement, you can erode your pension benefits.

Ms. Mutschler, also a professor at Brandeis University, suggests that women *manage their investment assets in retirement* by making sure their money will grow. Here's how: Avoid being a "bag lady" by investing small chunks of change daily. Write down each purchase on a small tablet you carry in your purse. Don't forget anything. Do this for two weeks and track your spending.

Gradually, certain spending patterns will emerge. Are

you buying Starbucks once a day? Do you take all your clothes to the cleaners? Do you buy your child an ice-cream after school? What about McDonald's? Do you buy candy or popcorn at the movies? You guessed it, all these items add up. Here's a list, from Kerry Hannon, of typical prices for these items:

- Starbucks—$3
- McDonald's Happy Meal—$5
- Lunch at local deli—$7 to $10
- Ice cream at Baskin-Robbins—$3

If you would give up these expenditures and put them in a sock drawer, here's what you'd save: At $18.00 a day for 300 days a year, in ten years you'll earn $54,000, and $108,000 in 20 years, without interest. These sums would be much larger if you figured in interest from stocks or an investment account.

Is your child insisting you stop at Wendy's on the way to ballet or soccer? After a long day at school, kids truly are hungry. Try curbing their hunger by keeping snacks in the car in a lunch box with a thermos, which also lets you bring cold juice and fruit. Also, provide some trail mix (a mixture of dried fruit, nuts, and raisins).

## AMY'S STORY

"I was extremely careful with our money. I had to be. It was all we had."

Tall and model-thin, Amy looks sleek and professional in a full-length wool coat with black leather gloves. Her demeanor is direct, displaying an air of poise and confidence. But looks can be deceiving. Amy's life has been anything but steady. She just puts on a good act.

After an abusive 10-year marriage, Amy fled from the constant chaos. One day, after an angry fight, her husband held her hostage at gunpoint for 24 hours. That did it. Waiting until he fell asleep from exhaustion, Amy frantically loaded her two children into her Suburban and raced out of town.

When she reached Tulsa, all the money Amy had was in her pocket. After moving into a tiny two-bedroom apartment, she found a job within a few weeks. It had flexible hours, allowing her to arrive home by 6:00 P.M. Like many single mothers, Amy discovered how difficult it was to stretch her paycheck to cover three people. Each evening, she prepared a nutritious meal from scratch. Avoiding more expensive, pre-packaged goods, she made dishes like meatloaf, lasagna, and macaroni and cheese.

"Mealtime has become a tradition," says Amy, who found that eating evening meals with her children, ages 9 and 11, provided a source of comfort to them. Not only was she spending quality time with her children, but she was also saving money by not eating out, not to mention saving energy and gasoline by cutting down on endless activities and errands.

## OTHER COST-CUTTING MEASURES

PLAN YOUR PURCHASES. Refrain from impulse shopping. Is it the beginning of school? Shop for school supplies or clothes in the summer at sale prices or in a discount store.

**SHOP AT GARAGE OR ESTATE SALES.** Did you know you can find usable clothes, books, and toys? And don't forget to haggle for a lower price.

**HAND-ME-DOWNS.** Don't be afraid to ask friends or relatives for hand-me-downs. Often, children barely wear some dresses or casual clothes. Blue jeans, T-shirts, and jackets are good bets, especially with younger children who aren't as tuned into fashion trends yet.

**COLLECT.** Other items for rainy-day activities: drawing paper, yarn, packing material, wrapping paper, ribbon, glue, scissors, and glitter. Place all these items in an easy-to-reach drawer. Presto! You've created an "art corner" where your child can play anytime. This beats buying an expensive toy, plus, you may be nurturing a Picasso!

**GIVE YOUR CHILD SPACE.** Provide a space where your child can get messy. If you set up a workspace, your child will often work on projects without asking for your help. Whether your children are making mud pies in the backyard, building a fort out of old Christmas trees, or hiding in an oversized cardboard box, they're exploring the world using their imagination.

**BAN TV COMMERCIALS.** They tend to brain-wash kids! By limiting TV watching, you'll also have more control over your child's purchases. Their appetites are whetted by commercials.

**HAIRCUTS.** Save on expensive haircuts by going to a

beauty school where trainees provide services for a reduced fee. Also, you may try this for coloring your hair or receiving a permanent or manicure.

KIDS' TOY SALES. Children can have their own sales where they get rid of old toys, videos, or books. And sell lemonade! If you teach them to take care of their things, the younger neighbors may love their "gently used" items. Plus, they'll be learning how to manage their own money.

## NOW'S THE TIME TO INVEST

Have you allowed yourself time to grieve? Now it's time to learn how to make your money work for you. Don't worry, no one's judging your financial savvy. Get together with a financial planner to come up with a *plan of action.* Remember, it's just a plan, not a lifetime commitment. As you create this plan, ask yourself: *what are my greatest needs?* College for my kids? Retirement savings? Emergency funds? Long-term care? As you create your goals, you'll develop spending priorities. Remember, this is *your* plan—not your financial planner's.

Consider your first encounter with financial planning as an education. Don't be afraid to ask questions about budgeting, goal setting, how to buy insurance, care-giving expenses, and how to locate important documents. You can find out about seminars on this subject by contacting your local American Association of Retired Persons (AARP), which sponsors the Women's Financial Information Program every Spring.

## TURNING OVER FINANCES
## TO SOMEONE ELSE

Some older women make the mistake of turning over their finances to another man just as they did with their husband. In Betty's case, she didn't want to think about finances, so she continued using her husband's stockbroker. After a few months, she discovered he had lost some $70,000 of her money. "I was mortified and hurt. This man was a good friend of my husband," she said. "Thank God he didn't touch my IRAs."

Since then, she's interviewed and selected a financial planner she works well with. One that's *her* choice.

## HIRING ATTORNEYS

The same goes for attorneys. Instead of sticking with your husband's "oldest friend," try selecting an attorney you may have a better rapport with. Someone you can talk to. Before you employ one, though, ask for a detailed accounting of fees and services. Be sure you know exactly what you're paying for. And clock your telephone conversations and personal time. Try keeping your emotions in check. You don't want to pay attorney's fees just for telling him what a bad day you had.

## DEAD-BEAT DADS

If you're worrying about your ex paying child support, the law is on your side. As of June 24, 1998, the U.S. Congress passed the Deadbeat Parents Punishment Act of

1998, which states that its purpose is "to establish felony violations for the failure to pay legal child support obligations and for other purposes." If your ex fails to pay child support, here's how to be prepared, according to financial consultant Kerry Hannon:

DOCUMENT YOUR DIVORCE AGREEMENTS. Make sure your divorce decree states the amount of the child care payments and when they are due each month. Keep records of when you receive them.

MISSING PAYMENTS? If he's consistently late on his payments, call your lawyer or a child support enforcement agency. Stop his behavior before it gets worse.

CREDIT BUREAU REPORTS. Report your ex to the credit bureau if he owes more than $1,000 in back payments. Federal law requires that child support enforcement agencies record anything due over $1,000.

BE BUSINESSLIKE, NOT EMOTIONAL. When dealing with dads-who-don't-pay, the calmer you are, the more control you have. Plus, as much as you think your husband is a failure, he's still your child's dad. "After all, he's your child's only father," says Ms. Hannon. "If they're bonded and *if their relationship is healthy*, it's best they continue this relationship. Don't bad-mouth dad in front of your child. Protect the feelings they have toward one another. Your child needs his dad. And, after a divorce, he needs him desperately."

LET'S LOOK AT KIT'S SITUATION. Thirteen years ago, she left her husband. She's only received child support for five of those years.

But she doesn't share her anger with her child. Each summer her child visits her ex and his grandparents because they are his family, too. "After Dustin visits his dad for the summer, he returns a different person," says Kit. "He's angry when I ask him to pick up his room, and he argues with me constantly. After a few weeks, though, he's back to normal." As children move from house to house, their schedules, as well as parents' rules and expectations, change, which causes confusion and chaos. But Kit knows how important it is for her son to visit his father. She refuses to share her anger with her son, because she knows he needs to trust his father.

At age 35, Mel divorced her husband when she found out about another woman in his life. With a 3-year-old child and little work experience, she was left helpless. When the child support ceased, she panicked. Her days were filled with rage. She remembers calling her ex's office, and castigating her own attorney when he failed to reach her husband.

But her anger didn't stop there.

One afternoon, as she picked up her 3-year-old up from school, she continued raving at her school teacher about her ex. The louder she spoke, the more quiet her child became. Suddenly, she stopped, because her child's eyes were filled with tears. "Mommy, why do you hate daddy?" she asked. Mel realized her anger needed to be channeled. Her rage only hurt those who loved her the most. She decided to fight her husband through legal methods, rather than emotional ones.

## DUMPING THE DEBT

If you're recovering from a divorce or death, you're in for lots of surprises. Consider the situation with Sue, 70.

Her entire life she loved her husband in spite of his erratic business decisions. In their marriage, he moved from California to Texas and back three times in ten years, looking for land in the development business. But she always supported him. As the mother of six children, her time was spent rearing them and tending to their home.

At his death, Sue discovered that her husband had left a $60,000 lien on her townhome. And although she desperately wanted to sell, she was stuck in a decaying neighborhood because of this burden.

Like Sue, many women find out that their spouses have not left them financially the way they expected. In fact, they realize that *there is no one who will look out for them like themselves.* So what did Sue do?

Instead of wasting her emotions on the problem, she got to work. She called her oldest son and offered him a good sum of money if he'd include her in one of his business deals. This brought her around $2,000 a month, which allowed her to eventually pay off the townhome lien.

In dire economic circumstances, we must hold our emotions in check. It's no time to "lose it." When you want something done, call a professional and work out a plan. You'll find there are solutions to the toughest problems.

## TRACK YOUR ASSETS

If you're like Sue, you may not realize what you're in for until it's almost too late. Unfortunately, if we turn over all business decisions to our spouses, we are also relinquishing control of our finances. This is a mistake. If we outlive our spouses, it leaves us in an untenable situation. *Dangerous* is a better word.

Is your spouse ailing? Are you separated from your spouse? Here's how to take control and track your assets:

- Study copies of the last three years of your tax return.
- Investigate what's in your safe deposit box. If you have safe deposit boxes in both your names, closely examine the contents. And take notes in the process.
- Check out last year's credit statements and insurance documents, including homeowner's, auto, life, and personal property.
- Call credit bureaus and ask for reports. Major credit bureau numbers are toll-free: Experian, 800-682-7654; Equifax, 800-685-1111; Trans-Union, 800-888-4213.

Why is it important to check out your spouse's or your soon-to-be ex's money records? Because money is a powerful tool and unless we are aware of our finances, we cannot protect ourselves.

## DAY TO DAY

What about your day-to-day debt? Are you between a rock and a hard place, where you owe your soul to credit card companies, retail stores, loans for college, or the mortgage company? Are you wondering how on earth you're going to dig out of this mess?

And, if you're going through a divorce, how do you free yourself from your husband's debt, such as credit cards held in joint names, for example? The solution is to get credit cards issued in your own name. Close out the old accounts and reopen *your own account in your own name.* And leave the indebted accounts in his name. You are still responsible for half of the old debt, but will avoid paying for his subsequent purchases. As you pay off your credit card monthly, you'll build up your credit history. Remember, don't miss any payments. A clear credit history is vital in case of divorce or death. You may need it to survive.

## ESTABLISHING A LINE OF CREDIT

Barbara Tom Jowell and Donnette Schwisow, authors of *After He's Gone,* suggest that all women need a line of credit at their bank to use in case of emergency. "Get a loan in your own name from the bank and pay it back in timely fashion, so the bank knows you're a good risk. You have to pledge collateral (some kind of property to leave with the bank) until the loan is paid off. But it still belongs to you, it's just pledged," Jowell and Schwisow explain.

## NEST-EGG STRATEGIES

Did you know that financial experts are encouraging women to develop a more aggressive strategy for building a nest egg? When it comes to investing, you're advised to get your feet wet. You could discover that jumping in may be safer than wading along the shore.

"This is not your mother's retirement," advises Pamela Ostuw, research analyst at the Employment Benefits Research Institute (EBRI), a Washington-based research organization. Many women ages 50 to 60 now find themselves in a new situation where the old rules for securing their future no longer apply.

In the past, our mothers relied on their husbands to provide economic security. But the women of the baby-boom generation and even some a little older face new challenges in preparing for retirement.

Some of these challenges are brought on by women outliving men. Others are caused by women caring for their ailing parents. The cost of caring for aging parents usually falls to the eldest female child, regardless of her economic status, says Phyllis Mutschler, executive director of the National Center on Women and Aging. This is another reason for women to learn more about investing and to prepare for long-term independence.

In fact, the AARP reports:

- Nearly one in five women ages 45 to 54 is now divorced and facing the prospect of beginning her retirement alone.
- Of all women ages 45 to 59 working full time in

the private sector today, 4 out of 10 have no pension with their current employer, according to the U.S. Department of Labor.

So, how do you prepare for financial independence? Start saving for retirement. That's what more women are doing. In fact, EBRI's annual Retirement Confidence Survey reported that 70 percent of women were actively saving for their retirement. That's up from 58 percent in 1994.

## HOW TO START SAVING

- Pay yourself first. Try investing $100 every month. At 8 percent, you'll accumulate nearly $35,000 in 15 years.
- If you're saving already, increase it. Did you know that 61 percent of women admitted that they could save an extra $20 a week by cutting back on eating out or entertainment? That's a fact, according to the Employee Benefits Research Institute.
- Does your employer match your 401(k) contributions? Then contribute to the max. If you change jobs, resist cashing out or dipping into your 401(k). Either roll it over into another tax-deferred investment vehicle or leave it where it is.

As you learn about your finances, you'll learn more about yourself. Your fears. Your values. Your treasures. Your dreams. Taking charge of your finances is not mysterious. It's not rocket science. But it is *vital* to your preservation and your independence.

### SUZE ORMAN SPEAKS OUT

Suze Orman, financial planner, lecturer, and author of the best-selling *Courage to be Rich*, which appeared on the *New York Times* Bestseller list, advises women on taking charge of their money.

#### MARRIED OR UNMARRIED WOMEN
- It is imperative to take charge of your money before an emergency arises. If you are experiencing a divorce or death, your heart is breaking and that is not the time to learn about money.
- Take care of your future by taking care of your todays.

#### DIVORCING?
If you haven't taken charge of your finances throughout the marriage, hire a tough attorney to help during the divorce procedure. Let him guide you. Be a warrior on the battlefield. You need help. You're not in any condition to fight this battle alone.

#### OVER 45?
- Middle-aged women need to realize they may outlive their spouse by ten to twenty years.

- The time to find out about your money is before a loss. You must take charge now.
- If you're in a relationship where your spouse
  resists you learning about money, that is a sign
  that he is also unsure of the money situation.
  Men who are secure about their finances usually want their wives to learn about money.
- If your husband resists setting up a will or
  trust, there's the chance he doesn't want to face
  up to his inability to manage his money successfully. Chances are, he doesn't want to face
  his mortality.

WHAT TO DO?

Make sure your affairs are in order. The more
arrangements you make now concerning funeral
arrangements, cremation, burial costs, and establishing a living will and trust, the fewer decisions you'll
have to make at the time of a death. These decisions
may be costly, and you will not be in the frame of
mind to think clearly about them.

WIDOWS?

It's never too late to take charge financially. Hiring a financial planner of your choosing, studying
your stocks and investments, and taking finance
courses prepare you to take charge. As soon as
women become financially educated, they take action.
They find themselves totally capable.

## CHAPTER 6 REVIEW: MIND YOUR MONEY MATTERS, AND YOU'LL BE HAPPIER FOR IT

- **Avoid letting someone else** handle your finances. Take charge!
- **Don't let grieving prevent you from planning** for your financial future.
- **Locate tax returns,** insurance policies, wills, and brokerage and bank accounts, and try working on each of these documents each day if you need to.
- **When you're ready,** interview several financial planners. Don't forget to check out their references and professional qualifications.
- **Shape a financial plan for yourself.** Not for your financial planner or your brother-in-law. Weigh each decision. Don't act hastily.
- **Arm yourself with financial information** by reading the *Wall Street Journal, Money, Business Week,* or *Success.* Also, read *Making the Most of Your Money* by Jane Bryant Quinn (Simon and Schuster, 1991).
- **Write down each purchase daily** for two weeks. Gradually, certain spending patterns will emerge.
- **Cost-cutters and -savers:** Plan your purchases. Refrain from impulse shopping. Shop at garage and estate sales. Ask friends for hand-me-downs.
- **Widows beware.** Although you may receive a lump sum of money from your husband's pension

or insurance, that money may have to last for the rest of your life.

- **Dealing with a funeral.** The earlier you make financial preparations for funeral expenses, the more time you will have to grieve unburdened by worry or distraction.

# say no and mean it

Learning to say "no" has been a lifetime struggle for Cleta, 58. Today, four years after the end of a painful 21-year marriage, she still has trouble ordering for herself in a restaurant.

After her divorce, Cleta left her teaching position and began selling insurance. Although she's made strides in her new career, she still suffers from self-esteem problems.

Unfortunately, many women suffering from loss act like Cleta. Lacking the confidence to decide what they do and don't want to do, at home and at work, is common for women.

## CUTTING THE TIES

And what if you have children in the marriage? It is difficult to cut the emotional ties, because you remain in contact with your ex.

Emotions don't cease just because a marriage dissolves.

As long as you continue to allow your ex to push your buttons, he'll be able to control you. And the more difficult it will be to *say no* to his demands.

Sylvia, a former model, is still learning to cut emotional ties with her ex.

Once a month, she faces him in a public place, where they have a "financial meeting." Armed with well-prepared notes, she states her case plainly. Looks him directly in the eye. "Although it's difficult, I try to maintain a distant relationship with Robert," says Sylvia, 44. "I talk to him as I would my CPA or my child's teacher. For my child's sake, he is someone important whom I have to interact with, but I will no longer allow him to push my emotional buttons."

This, however, takes practice.

Sylvia remembers a time when she'd flinch at her husband's finger-pointing and domineering attitude.

As a powerful attorney representing Fortune 500 clients, he used the same tactics at home as he did in the courtroom.

After 23 years, Sylvia filed for divorce, but the battle kept raging. Slowly, with the help of therapy, she started learning to *say no*. Two years after the divorce, Sylvia is learning to distance herself emotionally from her husband's criticisms. She uses humor when approaching him. And she's teaching her children to do the same.

"Over the past 15 years in America," writes Dr. Ken Dychtwald in his book *Age Wave* (Bantam, 1990), for every two marriages in a year, there is one divorce in that same year. Because of this, many individuals are now forced to emotionally disentangle themselves from their ex-spouses and begin anew.

In *Rebuilding—When Your Relationship Ends* (Impact, 1992), author Bruce Fisher points out to divorced individuals the importance of "taking out the trash, or dumping leftovers from your past life and love relationship."

A professional litigator, Sylvia opted to handle her divorce herself. "Instead of hiring an attorney, I handled the litigation," she says. "I wanted to set standards for my children. I didn't want them to see my husband and I fighting over money. I wanted them to see a crisis which we solved with dignity."

**Barbara, 48, advertising executive.** Barbara also finds it difficult but necessary to make a healthy break with her ex. "When you are joined at the hip with your ex, because of your child, disentangling is hard to do."

Divorced just eight months, Barbara has shared custody of their son, Temple. She found that "saying no" and setting boundaries with her ex are easier if she keeps conversations short and impersonal. "Having close contact with him on a daily basis puts my life in turmoil, and it makes it difficult for me to function," she explains. Despite the tension, Barbara never criticizes her ex in front of her son. She believes that it's wrong for her 4-year-old child to be put in the middle of fighting parents.

Barbara also encourages her son to continue seeing his paternal grandmother on a regular basis. "Although his father and I are divorced, I would never interfere with Temple's relationship with his grandmother. He needs all the family contact he can get now," she says.

Marriage and family counselor Bruce Drobeck says that before you can set boundaries, you need to break the ties with your ex. But a legal divorce does not necessarily mean individuals are emotionally separated.

Often, there is a tug-of-war between ex-spouses. Some couples continue destructive behavior patterns which began early in the marriage.

**Nan, soft-spoken, poised.** With ash-blonde hair, Nan dresses comfortably in Birkenstock sandals and thick socks. She wears a peasant blouse with a long skirt, looking like a college professor. It's surprising to learn she heads a commercial electrical company.

For 28 years, Nan worked with her husband as his bookkeeper, then later as his financial adviser. During this time, the company grew from six people to over 30. In spite of the company's progress, Nan received little recognition for her work. Like all his employees, her husband usually ridiculed her in front of others. He would often burst out, "Godammit-Nan-what-do-you-think-you're-doing!" Or, if she left in the heat of an argument and went to the bathroom, he'd follow her there and bang on the door. Through the years, Nan accepted this behavior. In fact, she often felt like she was the cause of his outbursts. But, as the company grew, her husband began to lose interest in the firm on a day-to-day basis, preferring to travel and go to conferences. The daily decisions fell on Nan. And the more responsibility she assumed, the more confident she became.

The year she was selected as president of her trade organization, she filed for divorce. "I realized that if others recognized me for my leadership skills and business savvy, then staying in an empty relationship was destructive to my future, and to the future of my children."

With new-found confidence, she was able to stand up to her husband. But she was still learning to say "no."

Two years after the divorce, Nan endured the last of her husband's yelling. After one of his outbursts, she said that his behavior was upsetting their employees, and that he should refrain from coming to the office on a daily basis. "You've run this company for a dozen years, and I'd like to try my hand at it."

Like Sylvia, she stated her case plainly and didn't budge. She arranged to meet with her ex-husband once a month and give him a financial update on the company. "He knew I was serious," she says. "And he depended on me. If I left the company, it would be in serious jeopardy."

With time, Nan took over the company and bought her ex-husband out. At this point, they had been divorced for five years. The day she bought him out was the day she felt her divorce was actually final. "It provided me with much-needed closure," she explains. "For the first time in my life, I was free."

Psychologists say that breaking the tendency to allow others to "push our emotional buttons" is difficult. They believe you should not dwell too long in any stage of recovery where you experience feelings of denial, anger, loss, pain, or guilt.

If you spend an inordinate amount of time thinking about your ex or being angry, this will prevent you from getting on with your life.

After interviewing 60 families of divorce over 15 years, authors Judith S. Wallenstein and Sandra Blakeslee comment on how difficult it is to establish an emotional distance from ex-spouses.

In their book *Second Chances* (Ticknor and Fields, 1990), they say there is no evidence that time automatically diminishes feelings or memories; that hurt or depression are overcome; or that jealousy, anger, and outrage will vanish.

"People go on living, but just because they have lived 10 years or more does not mean they have recovered from hurt," the authors say.

People are more likely to succeed after divorce if they have some history of competence, the authors say, or some earlier reference points to serve as a reminder of independence and success.

Recovery is an active process, they say, and involves active effort, planning, and the ability to make constructive use of new options and to move ahead.

Six years after her divorce, Sylvia has increased her work as a professional litigator. She handles her clients with ease and has learned to communicate more efficiently with her ex-husband. "After years of feeling like I was jumping through hoops to meet my husband's emotional demands, it is nice to feel free and in control," she says.

## SELF-ASSERTION

One way to put an end to emotional confrontations is to be more assertive. And that means speaking up even if you risk making a fool of yourself. Clinical psychologist Pamela Butler says women may have this problem because they were raised to concentrate on nurturing and life-preserving activities and "to live through and for others, rather than ourselves."

Dr. Butler, a resident of Marin County, California, says

that in today's culture, women tend to block their ability to be assertive by what they tell themselves. Our "internal dialogue" creates negative self-labels, found in phrases like:

- "If people get to know me, I won't measure up."
- "I'm afraid someone will think I'm not intelligent, so I won't give my opinion."
- "I have trouble saying what I want or need. Someone may think I'm too demanding and they won't like me."

When Maggie and her husband fought, he often resorted to name-calling. "You're just crazy!" was his familiar phrase—"go take a tranquilizer!" After a few years of this, Maggie started believing her husband. She thought she did need tranquilizers. It never occurred to her that being branded "crazy" was unfair and untrue. Unfortunately, instead of fighting fairly, most men fight to win. And if they have to put you down, they will.

But you don't have to buy into this behavior.

The next time you hear someone refer to you in terms like *nagging, cold, unresponsive, unimportant, menopausal, too idealistic,* or *emotional,* don't believe them. And, certainly, don't apply these negative words to yourself. If you do, it will guarantee that you lose the next argument.

### Facial Expressions

According to Dr. Butler, an assertiveness training expert, self-assertion is also shown through facial expressions. She points out that some women are afraid to show their feelings for fear of rejection, so they respond with a blank face. This is because anger, resentment, and annoyance traditionally have not been considered appropriate feminine emotions.

### Assertive vs. Aggressive

"I" messages are assertive, continues Dr. Butler. For example,

- "I feel."
- "I resent."
- "I am angry."

"I" messages convey that "I have feelings and my feelings are my own responsibility." In contrast, aggressive expressions usually involve "you" messages, leading to a counterattack or defense. A "you" message feels like an intrusion. Alternatively, "I" messages offer no intrusion or put-down.

An "I" message (stating one's feelings), rather than a "you" message (conveying an attack), is more effective. It allows you to respond assertively rather than aggressively.

### Why Not Respond Aggressively?

For many women, says Dr. Butler, aggressive expression leaves a "bitter aftertaste." After the anger subsides, you may feel guilty or regretful, thinking, "'Why did I have to explode?'"

If you want to win an argument, it's best to learn how to be assertive. It will guarantee having people respect you and ultimately agree with you. Aggressiveness, on the other hand, only creates resentment and fear, leading to a constant battle.

But how do we do this? Women are traditionally conditioned to be non-assertive. And newly single women may have it even harder. As we separate from our spouses, either through divorce or death, we are anxious. We don't know what's expected. The rules are unclear, and we live with ambiguity and doubt.

## SAYING "NO" IN THE WORKPLACE

Let's face it. We all hate being called a "bitch" and we'll go to any lengths to prevent it.

In the 1950s, our mothers taught us to be "ladylike." In the 1960s, as hippies, we wore long dresses and beads, pretending to be more interested in sex than in politics. And in the new millennium, we're still hesitant to step on anyone's toes.

Maybe women are conditioned to be non-assertive. But what does this mean? If a man is determined, strong, and a perfectionist, he's labeled "powerful." If a woman has the same qualities, she's labeled a "bitch." Women are criticized if they exhibit strong traits. Some are called "ball-breakers."

**IS YOUR WORKPLACE ALIENATING YOU?**

Even if you don't agree with your co-workers, it's good to be *aware of their feelings*. If you're getting the cold shoulder in your office, maybe you should ask yourself:

- Are my office-mates excluding me from their projects?
- Am I being alienated from other co-workers?
- Do people talk to me freely?
- What are the expressions on their faces when I come into a room? Are they free and open?

If people *are* avoiding you, perhaps you need to change your attitude. Maybe you *are* acting like a bitch!

SOURCE: Financial adviser and iVillage.com columnist Kerry Hannon

---

### Saying "No" to Your Boss

Your boss is unbearable. He's dumping on you for the third time this week. He drops impossible deadlines in your lap, expecting immediate turnaround. He's rude. Abrasive. And temperamental. Plus, he's refused to raise your salary for the last year. What do you do? Is he going through a bad time? Is the company declining? Is his wife leaving him?

Whatever it is, you need to address it. But how? *Very*

*gently.* If he expresses an opinion, listen with an open mind and respond with clarity. Attempt to empathize with others as well as yourself, says consultant and professional speaker David Eastman in *The Idiot's Guide to Assertiveness* (Alpha Books, 1997).

Before you say "no" to your boss, instead of rushing into his office, prepare yourself for the meeting. You may have more leverage than you think, says Davidson, if you follow these tactics.

Before visiting your boss, boost your confidence by listing your positive qualities. You'll need them!

- List your specific skills. Your positive skills.
- List the empowering people in your life, like mentors, coaches, teachers, parents, friends, advisors, team members, and helpers.
- When you've completed the list, put it away and go on retreat. Wait another day and review the list.

In addition to preparing a resource list, don't forget to follow these tips:

- Compliment the boss. He needs recognition too.
- Gather your evidence.
- Do your homework. Back up points with statistical information or cost benefits.
- Keep your emotions in check. Don't dump on the boss.
- Use "we" or "us" phrasing instead of "I" or "my." Use "team references."

- Don't shirk responsibility. Don't blame other departments for wrongdoing unless those departments are actually at fault.
- Present the problem clearly and move on. Remember, your boss's time is valuable.

### Delivering Bad News? Try This Strategy

- Start with some good news.
- Give the bad news, and follow it with some possible solutions.
- End with some other good news.

### Saying "No" to More Work

Refrain from using "I'm sorry." try:

- "I would like to accept that project, but I don't think it would be in our best interest since I'm already involved on the ABC project."
- "I'm maxed out right now. If I take on this project, I'm afraid I won't be able to give it my best effort."

### Kate's Story

On Kate's first sales job, she didn't hesitate to say "no" to her boss when it came to her 8-year-old daughter. As part of her sales training, Kate, a divorcee, had to be in the office at 7:30 A.M. In her rush to get to work, she didn't notice that it was still dark outside due to a recent time change. "I'll never forget. I dropped Loren off at the school, but it was still closed. I drove off leaving my child sitting on the steps, in the dark," says Kate, 47, her eyes filling, "I can still see her sitting there, dressed in her little school uniform. Oh God, it was awful."

When Kate reached her office, tears were streaming down her face. She marched into her boss's office saying, "I can't do this again. I'll never leave my daughter like that again."

As luck would have it, the boss agreed to help her out. He hired a college student to take her daughter to school during the training session. But Kate was determined to not make allowances for her boss. If he'd complained, she was prepared to quit her job.

## SAYING "NO" TO YOUR KIDS

Louise, 46, had trouble saying no to her 17-year-old daughter. "Three years ago, my daughter ruled the house," Louise said. "When she complained about being unhappy, I felt responsible. And, because I wanted to make her happy, I had a difficult time saying no to her."

"When I'd ground her, she would apologize, and then I'd give in," says Louise, who is divorced. "My ex was more authoritative, which I resented. He made me look ridiculous."

After family counseling, Louise, a teacher, learned to compare her daughter to her own pupils. "Although teens may be adult-looking in their appearance, they need the same limits as a small child," she says. "I learned to say, 'No, enough discussion,' and then I'd leave the room."

Sharon Scott, a marriage and family counselor, also believes that mothers get dumped on because they have difficulty saying "no."

Ms. Scott, who conducts parenting workshops for school districts throughout the nation, advises women to avoid arguing with their children. "Once you say 'no,' end the conversation and walk away. If you can't say 'no' to your child, how can you expect to say 'no' to others?" she asks.

"Burnout occurs when we don't replenish ourselves. When we learn to take care of ourselves," adds Ms. Scott, "then we are ready to say 'no'—comfortably."

Dr. Garry Landreth, a psychologist and director of the Center for Play Therapy at the University of North Texas, also suggests that mothers should learn to say "no" by developing their self-esteem. "In disciplining children, the exact words are not necessarily what is important. It's the presentation of those words. If a child feels the mother has a wishy-washy tone or manner, then the child will continue to push and ignore the mother's request."

One way for women to boost their self-esteem is to give themselves affirming messages such as "taking care of myself is good" and "I'm not responsible for the feelings of others."

Remember to stay calm. If you appeal to the best part of an individual, you are more likely to get a cooperative reaction.

Gay Jurgens is a marriage and family therapist who teaches women to say "no" in her course, "Assertiveness and Awareness for Singles," offered nationwide.

"We need to have a nice, sturdy fence with a gate around us to protect our garden," she says. "When we learn to say 'no,' we are exercising the muscle that opens and closes the gate."

Through Ms. Jurgen's course, Cleta, 58 and divorced, says she's discovered a new confidence in her profession and in her inner self.

"I've learned that it's okay to do things for me," she says. "Unless I tell others what I need, how will they ever know?"

## DATING AND SAYING "NO"

Assertiveness doesn't end in the work place or at home. One of the most important places to assert yourself is when you are dating.

Dating is complicated, especially after a death or divorce. Many of us are new to the dating scene. And through the years, the rules have changed.

But there's one thing that's stayed the same: Your freedom to say "no."

According to Ms. Jurgens, many women are afraid of saying "no" from the get-go. They accept dates with people they're not interested in, because they're afraid of hurting someone's feelings.

On a date, she adds, some of these same women also refuse to say "no" to a man's sexual advances for the same reason.

Some won't remove a hand from their breast for fear of making a scene, says Ms. Jurgens. Why are women so fearful of saying "no" to sex? Many are conditioned to give in to a man's advances, even if they are not attracted to him.

## ARE ASSERTIVE WOMEN COLD?

According to Pamela Butler, psychologist, there is
a common belief directed at women: Assertive
women are cold, castrating bitches. If I'm assertive,
I'll be so unpleasant that people won't like me.

## ASSERTIVENESS AND SEX

In addition to saying "no" to unwelcome sex, many
women are reluctant to relax and enjoy sex with someone they care for. Call it shy. Call it inhibited. Whatever
it is, it comes from holding back feelings. And it comes
from lacking trust in relationships.

If you're newly divorced, you may be thought of as
hungry for sex, or asking for sexual advances.

If you're ready for a sexual experience, expressing
what you want and do not want should be natural to you.

Try not to judge each sexual experience. Don't analyze
it as a performance. That will kill all spontaneity. And remember, giggling and laughing are permitted in the bedroom. Be able to laugh at your foibles. There's no such
thing as "perfect sex." The faster you move the Olympics
out of the bedroom, the more fun you'll have.

With a person you love, sex is a trusting, sensual "happening."

Experts say the key to sexual communication is laughter and play. This visualization exercise may help as well:

*Close your eyes and pretend* your bed is a desert island,

## ASSERTIVENESS *IS* GOOD

Assertive women are direct and honest and behave appropriately. They show a genuine concern for other people's rights and feelings, as well as their own. Their assertiveness enriches their relations with others.

where you meet your lover for the first time. Carefree days are spent eating pineapples, swimming in blue lagoons, and lying in the sun. Each night you build a big fire and make love in the moonlight.

## SPEAK YOUR MIND

Saying "no" to others, whether it's your boss, your children, your lover, or your ex, occurs when you have *confidence*—when you aren't afraid to speak your mind. But this is difficult when you are newly separated, says Arthur Kovacs, a Santa Monica psychologist. "We become anxious when the rules are unbroken," he says. "When we don't know what's expected of us, and how we're to conduct ourselves."

You have to shift your needs for intimacy and kindness, for understanding and support, from your ex to a new cast of characters as soon as possible, says Dr. Kovacs. Shift to a support group, co-workers, church, friends, or group therapy participants.

This change often takes time and during the process, we may find ourselves isolated and alone.

As you work through this transition, your confidence may be the first to go. As you deal with your situation, you may hide from others, until you work things out. The result: Isolation may lead to a sense of failure.

The key to asserting yourself is knowing what you want. And being able to assess your priorities. In short, some issues are worth fighting for, some are not. For example, personal issues are health, finances, intellect, and welfare. Professional issues: Loyalty, tenacity, integrity, or follow-through.

## REMEMBER

Whatever you do when selecting priorities, remember to keep the number manageable. The fewer the priorities, the more energy and effort you can lend to each of them.

Author Jeff Davidson says that the more self-confident you are, the clearer it becomes when you need to assert yourself. And the more self-confident you are, the less often you need to be assertive. The highly self-confident person who experiences a put-down may not feel compelled to respond in kind. Achieving an "assertive balance" is probably the most admirable trait you can have.

When it comes to living alone, learning to express your feelings about important issues is key to your survival.

Saying "no" nicely, but firmly and consistently, paves the way to independence.

When a woman *states her feelings as fully as possible,* she is being assertive. This is equally true whether the feeling is expressed in anger or affection. Statements such as "I feel annoyed," "I resent what you just said," or "I am furious at you" are all assertive statements.

On the other hand, some aggressive statements are, "You're really immature." "You're a slob," and "If you were a good person, you wouldn't do that."

As you can see, assertive statements express what is being felt at the moment. But aggressive statements sound more like an attack. Learning *when* to say "no" is as vital as *how* to say it. Choose your battles wisely. Think before speaking. Take time to react. And pace your response.

It may be your last chance.

## CHAPTER 7 REVIEW: YES, YOU CAN BE HAPPIER SAYING "NO"

- **Say "no" with confidence.** Don't be afraid to speak your mind.
- **Be assertive.** Know what you want. Choose your battles wisely.
- **Say "I."** Avoid using "you always," which accuses others of wrongdoing. Instead, use "I" language, like "I feel," "I resent," or "I'm angry."
- **Is your ex pushing your emotional buttons?** Stop it with an emotional "no" by approaching him calmly. Remember, it takes two to have a tug-of-war.
- **Avoid putting your child in the middle.** Keep your child out of emotional battles with your ex. Your child needs to be sure of his dad's love.

- **How to say "no" to your boss.** Don't rush into a meeting. Bring up points with statistics and cost benefits to back up your position.
- **How to say "no" to your kids.** Once you say "no," end the discussion and walk away. The longer you argue, the better their chance of talking you out it. Or into it.
- **Don't be afraid to say "no" to dates.** Don't accept a date with a person you don't like. Don't be afraid to reject *any* or *all* sexual advances.
- **Delivering bad news?** Avoid saying, "I'm sorry." Use positive statements and explanations like, "I would like to take this project, but I don't think I can give it my best at this time."
- **Seek counseling.** If you're stuck and have trouble establishing boundaries, trouble saying "no," seek the benefit of a professional counselor or psychologist who can offer guidance.

# daring to date again

The divorce is final. You've done your grieving. You long for male companionship and a little romance, but are you ready?

Although you may feel ready, chances are you're not. If you're getting over a divorce, you may feel lonely, or you may confuse falling in love with receiving warmth from another person, or indulging in intimacy or sex. You may also find yourself loving the idealized image of a person rather than a real person, especially if you've been hurt in a previous relationship.

If you haven't known unconditional love from your parents or your former lovers, then you have to learn to love yourself first, before you can love others.

That's why it's wise to avoid getting involved too soon after a divorce. Play it safe, develop platonic friendships, and take it slow.

Mary is an example. After leaving her alcoholic husband, she chose to share male companionship in the safe environment of her church singles group. Here, she went out with dozens of gals and guys—always in a group. "I wasn't ready to date seriously," she says. "But I did enjoy my male friends. We shared laughter, tears, and lots of hugs, with no strings attached."

According to Dr. Bruce Fisher, more mature love will grow if people can move beyond loving idealized images of each other. "Looking for love often keeps real lovers away," he says. He states that what we lack in ourselves, we often try to find in another individual. If you're suffering a loss, learning to love yourself first is imperative. It helps you heal your wounds. And it helps you appreciate real love, when it occurs.

Whether you are newly divorced or widowed, recognize the importance of caring for yourself first, through therapy, friendships, or support groups. "Your goal for now is to get acquainted and develop friendships with the people around you," says Dr. Fisher. "Pay no attention to whether or not they are 'eligible singles.' Notice only if they are interesting people you would like to get to know."

As you create positive relationships with both sexes, you will begin to attract people who can help you heal. As you go through this process, be kind to yourself. The initial healing process allows us to replenish ourselves by feeling pleasure through taste, touch, sight, and sound. This may be better than throwing ourselves into another's arms.

With time, we may want to look for a partner. But, if we've focused on nurturing ourselves first, we may not have to "go hunting"—that person may come about naturally. After all, good friends make the best lovers.

## SELF-CARE

If you're feeling lost or empty, pay attention to yourself. Replenish yourself:

- Sit in the sun for ten minutes a day.
- Light candles and say a silent prayer for a better day. Go through this ritual daily.
- Paint a picture to the music of Mozart.
- Dance to your favorite Broadway musical soundtrack.
- Teach the dog a new trick.
- Go on a nature hike.
- Picnic in the park alone.
- Write in your journal.

## SUGGESTIONS FROM OTHER WOMEN

**Pat, 48.** "I carried around a little notebook in my purse. Every time I was feeling low, I'd write a line in it. It may be a prayer. A meditation. An affirmation. Or a cheerful word or action. Every time I heard something inspiring, I'd make note of it. After my divorce, I was so desperate to sort through my feelings, this was my way of building back my hope."

**Karen, 42.** "When I was missing my husband, I got in his bass boat and went fishing. I could sit on the lake in Minnesota for several hours, thinking of Peter and our love of the water. When we fished together, it was quiet and tranquil, and we found that we couldn't stay mad at each other. After his death, it was just the same. While fishing, I'd talk to him, telling him how difficult it was without him. Somehow, I could feel my husband listening to me. At the end of the day, I'd forget how angry I was over losing him. The water soothed me. I'd come home refreshed and relaxed."

**Nan, 53.** "I'm not sure how I worked through my husband's continual abuse. His insulting words would make me feel small, like a guilty child. In order to escape from him, I joined business organizations in the community. When I became national president of our trade organization, I gained a new confidence. I realized if others recognized my talents, then I must be one smart cookie, something my husband had never, never admitted."

**Molly, 78.** Molly lived in western Kentucky prior to the second World War. "I got through my darkest days by staying busy. After my husband left, I had no money and no way to pay the rent. My three children and I moved into a two-bedroom apartment, where we lived with my parents. A few months later I got a secretarial job, but soon, things got even worse when my parents became ill. My mother had heart trouble and my father had a stroke, all within a few months of each other. In spite of the hard times, though, I never looked back. A child of the Depression, I never thought anyone would save me, except myself. In time, though, I got involved in the town's community theater, where I honed my craft as an actress. This was my escape. It kept me going—and growing as an adult and an artist."

**Kate, 51.** "When I was eager to meet men, I had a party. I sent invitations to the single parents in my child's high school, inviting them to a wine and cheese party.

Unfortunately, only one person showed up. But it didn't bother me. I've been dating him for the last two years, and he's fabulous!"

## MISSING A WARM BODY

Are you missing the warmth of his embrace and touch? After a death or divorce, it's normal to feel this way. Even if the marriage wasn't perfect, you tend to remember the way it was when you first married. You remember the fresh scent of his just-shaved face. His tender touch. His sweet kisses.

Take Joan. After losing her husband to cancer, she was so anxious, she ached. "I felt like going up to a stranger in the street and asking him to hold me."

If you're in this state, you're wondering if romance might someday be a reality again. But before you start your search, give yourself a little more time. Try a manicure, a pedicure, a massage, or an oil bath by candlelight. If you like water, try swimming several times a week, or if you're a sun goddess, sunbathe in the nude (don't forget your sunscreen). Do something risky. Do something passionate. Something for yourself—your sensual self.

Successful healing involves being kind to ourselves. The initial healing process allows us to replenish ourselves *and* our loved ones. Allowing ourselves to feel pleasure through taste, touch, sight, and sound helps us to fill our emptiness. This may be better than getting intimate with someone before we're ready.

## WHEN YOU'RE READY FOR ROMANCE

If you've done your healing appropriately (six months to a year), you will attract healthy relationships. Remember, if you have a positive attitude, you will attract others who feel good about themselves. Don't look for potential marriage partners. Look for friends. People that you have something in common with. People who are uncritical, confident, and who have found happiness and send out those vibrations.

But how will you actually find a date?

Here are some safe, public places to meet someone: a beach, museum, park, church, theater, restaurant, community college class, or in activities like softball, folk dancing, gourmet cooking, traveling, hiking, acting, poetry readings, literature festivals, writing workshops, and more. Look into organizations like the Widowed Persons Service, Young Republicans or Democrats, Public Television, local senior citizens organizations, or Parents Without Partners.

It's good to do a little analysis before attending an activity. Make sure it is one that interests you, not just one where you'll meet someone. And when you arrive, don't just stick with your female friends. Chat with the men, they won't bite. Talk to all of the men—not just the most attractive. Be friendly. Don't obsess about finding "dating material." Have fun. Maybe you'll meet a good friend who may introduce you to others.

## AFTER YOU'VE FOUND HIM, THEN WHAT?

Dark-haired Betty Lucas lost her husband at 53. Three years later, she went to her monthly widowed-persons meeting where there were 200 women and "five men who were breathing."

This was a special day for her. As the new president of the organization, she stepped up to the podium to welcome the members. Across the room, she eyed a tall, handsome man, who was well over six feet tall. "Instantly, I was attracted to him, because of his height," says Betty, who is 5'10" tall.

After the meeting, she whispered to her friend, "Let's ask him out for coffee with our friends."

The invitation was successful, and Betty and Al have been together ever since.

How did she get the nerve to do this? "I've never been shy," she says laughing. "What did I have to lose? We were going for coffee anyway. I thought it would be nice to include him."

## RE-ENTERING THE DATING SCENE

Some of us aren't as brave as Betty. When you see an interesting man, you may not have the nerve to approach him. But through blind dates, friends, parties, singles organizations, community college classes, church, cultural events, or charity functions, you may land your first date.

What about the bars? Stay out of them. They are no place to meet an eligible man. Most people who hang out at bars are as desperate as they look.

## NOW WHAT?

Remember, dating should be fun, not a trial. If you relax and enjoy the moment, you'll enjoy your date more. Dating after a loss is for fun—not forever! It's good to maintain a little mystery. Don't reveal the details of your past romances, your lovers, or your divorce. Don't talk about your ailments. And don't share your most serious problems. Remember, a date offers a break from reality. Do what you can to make it light and relaxing. If you like your date, show your appreciation by laughing at his jokes or touching his arm. Take your time. Don't judge him. Enjoy each other.

## TAKE A BREAK FROM DATING

If you're not newly single, perhaps you've been dating for years. Are you tired of the games, the phony flirting? Pretending to have a good time when you're bored to death? Anna had reached that point. One day she decided that she wouldn't date for a year. No dates, no sex. "Celibacy looked good at that point," she admitted. Anna didn't expect much from the dating break, but she was surprised.

In that one year, she learned a lot about herself and her children. Through spending time alone writing poetry, she came to forgive her alcoholic parents for neglecting her as a child. In doing so, she also learned to forgive herself for the pain she brought to her children by her divorce. Without dating, the pace of her life changed. She didn't rush home from work, change clothes, and run out again with dates who were often forgettable. Instead, she hung out with her 9-year-old son, shooting baskets on the weekend. Chatted with her teenage daughter at midnight. Instead of shaping her schedule between her job, dating, and her kids, Anna had more time for herself, and she found this experience liberating. She found that her free time was her own.

She "celebrated" her celibacy by turning her house into something personal. She painted her bedroom the color of ripe peaches, hanging Picasso prints from the walls. She reupholstered her mother's antique chaise lounge in a soft velvet fabric, and spent hours there reading and writing. When her children were staying with her ex, Anna enjoyed the quiet. "For years, I'd shared my life with others," she says. "Now it was my time to be alone. I loved it. And I learned so much about myself. It was a peaceful time."

A year later, Anna went back to dating. Much stronger and better grounded, within a few months, she met "the man of her dreams." He was a gentle neurologist, who had a love for music and literature. Over a year later, Anna and Nathan married. They now share their lives happily.

## FEARING THE FUTURE?

Are you frightened of being alone? Do you feel like you're going to be alone for the rest of your life?

Take a year off to get yourself on your feet. At the end of the year, you'll feel a whole lot better. Then, if a man comes along, you'll be more adept at making good choices. You'll be able to tell whether or not you want to become part of a couple or stay single. Who knows? You may choose the latter.

How should you spend the year? Take this time for yourself. You may even discover you don't need a man to make you happy. No one can make you happy but yourself.

## HOW DATING AFFECTS KIDS

Although you may be ready for a new relationship, your children may not be. They won't tell you why they feel uncomfortable with your dating. But they may make their feelings known by their actions, like not giving you phone messages, being rude to your dates, or whining when you have company.

Why do they do this? Because they are still dealing with the grief of their loss, too. If your child is acting out, be patient. And reassure him of the fact that another man (your date) won't replace their father.

Their adjustment to your dating will take time but they'll eventually come around.

**Grace, 45, had the perfect solution.** She didn't let her child meet her dates at first. "I arranged for my daughter to stay with my sister on my date nights," she said. "Until I'd dated someone seriously for several months, I wouldn't introduce him to my daughter. I didn't want to parade men through my daughter's life unnecessarily."

**Genny took the opposite approach.** After dating Tom for three months, she allowed him to move in with her. After a few weeks, he lost his job and began drinking. As the drinking progressed, Genny asked him to leave, but her son was already attached to him. And he felt lost when Tom left abruptly.

"This type of situation is extremely difficult for children," says Mike Smith, a psychologist. "Having relationships is important, but don't drag them into your home unless you're sure of them."

## WATCH OUT FOR REVENGE DATING

Let's face it. Breaking up with someone you care for is never easy. When you've been through a divorce or death, you're quite vulnerable. Some people, both men and women, resort to "revenge dating" after they've been dumped by someone they care for.

Dr. Roger Rhoades, a divorce expert, says that revenge dating is more common in men, because they often have a difficult time admitting to being hurt in a relationship. When a man is hurt, he sometimes tries to hurt someone else in an act of revenge. "While a man is deep in the middle of revenge dating, part of the ritual is to become physically involved with as many women as possible. To make the revenge date complete," he continues, "many men do not take the time or even care about protecting themselves or the women they're with against sexually transmitted diseases."

So be careful when you're dating. Take time to get to know another person. And don't get sexually intimate for several months. To avoid AIDS, many couples have an AIDS blood test before they have intercourse or practice oral sex. And don't think that if you're over sixty, you don't have to worry about AIDS. White males over 60 are one of the fastest-growing populations to contract AIDS. Why? Because they don't use protection. Protect yourself—HIV can strike anyone, at any age, any time.

## ROCKY ROMANCES

Seated in the back of the restaurant, the couple seem oblivious to others. Their faces shimmer in the candlelight. As the woman sips her wine, her eyes never leave his face.

Suddenly, her beeper goes off.

Startled, the man looks at her and says, "You're not going to take that call, are you?"

"Of course I am," she says sweetly but firmly. "I'm not about to lose a sale."

He looks away, sighing. Tension fills his face as his mood swiftly changes.

**Cynthia, real estate agent.** She's meeting challenges in her relationships. But after being married twice in 17 years, she's not surprised. "Men can't stand me working on the weekends. It's okay if *they* need to work, but they don't have the patience for *my* work."

At this rate, she doubts if she is ever going to find "Mr. Right." She is not alone. For women who eventually do remarry, there is a 75 percent divorce rate. According to author Ken Dychtwald in his book *Age Wave* (Bantam Books, 1990), there are now five times as many widows as widowers, and fully half of all women over 65 are widows.

But *you* can beat these odds. It takes constant hard

work, and tapping into advice from friendly experts can't hurt. They can help us uncover and throw out past behaviors that work against long-term relationships.

Here are tips to take to heart. Courtship is divided into three parts, says therapist Kay King.

**1. Best foot forward.** Couples talk and talk. Share events and experiences. They are very interested in getting to know one another. If they engage in sex too soon, though, this stage will end prematurely, because a physical relationship overrides the emotional and intellectual.

**2. Tell it like it is.** Stage 2 is coming clean. It's when you say how you really feel about things. You know, like fessing up that you're sick of baseball after going to the stadium for months with great enthusiasm.

**3. Shall we dance?** If you survive Stage 2, then you are ready to dance, to make the commitment, but even at this juncture, you may decide that cultural or spiritual differences might rule marriage out. It is possible that we can love lots of people and still not want to marry them.

Are you attracted to the wrong person? There may be a reason. Perhaps you are choosing a person for the wrong reasons. Maybe you're attracted to his personality, not his character.

Good looks, a new car, a high-paying job, charm—these are the traits many people are drawn to, but these traits have little to do with character. Singles forget to notice character traits like: Does he pay his bills on time? How does he handle anger? How does he treat others?

In the courtship, we tend to minimize those day-to-day actions that make up character. We also mistakenly think the negative traits will magically disappear.

**Amy, 52, agrees.** A native of Franklin, Louisiana, she

once suffered from the "Southern belle syndrome," insisting on having a handsome, affluent man on her arm. "Now, I am looking for someone who has integrity and a sense of humor . . . not someone to take care of me. I'm looking for someone to share my life."

In addition to being aware of underlying character traits rather than surface charm, couples need good skills for resolving conflict or frustration for a relationship to last, according to relationship experts, who say that when couples get into conflict, they stop listening to each other. They become intent on being *heard* rather than *being quiet and listening*. They make the assumption, "if you don't give me what I want, you are being mean to me."

If you're interested in finding the "right person," you may consider attending or conducting a relationship workshop offered through your community or your church. At this workshop, try this exercise: Ask each individual to study their "relationship history" and its patterns, making a list of all the people they've been attracted to and the positive and negative traits of each.

Next, the individuals are asked to create a "want list" focusing on what they want to experience and how they want to feel in the relationship.

## RED FLAGS

As you date others, don't forget to pay attention to the red flags. Listen to your inner self. Even though you may be dating a doctor—a gorgeous, wealthy one—if that person is totally into himself, does not listen, and interrupts you, he may make you feel inadequate.

Also, ignoring long-term danger signals like alcoholism, drug abuse, or put-downs can be disastrous. If you say "don't treat me that way" and he ignores you . . . don't think for one minute that once you are married he will change.

When Sharon, 36, fell in love with her second husband, she was determined to know the truth about him. So she asked his first wife. "I found out what I'd expected," she says—"that he was a generous, creative, dynamic person. But that he was also a dismal failure at managing money."

In spite of being alerted to his "red flags," she consented to marry on one condition: That he agree to make her his business partner, allowing her to manage his finances.

## SEARCHING FOR MR. RIGHT

Kim, 38, a nutrition instructor, thought the search for "Mr. Right" was almost futile. Although divorced for four years, she didn't seriously begin looking until recently. She wondered if she'd ever meet the right person. "I thought there was a possibility that I'd never marry."

Then she met Aaron, 28, a designer, whom Kim describes as an extrovert.

"I've been shy all my life, so when I first met Aaron, it was difficult for me," she says. He first asked her to play racquetball, a safe approach for Kim. "I have confidence when I'm in a sports-type situation," she explains.

Two months later, it was tennis. After waiting for three months, because he was involved with someone else, Aaron finally asked her to dinner, and things took off from there.

It turned out that the combination of her shyness and his outgoing personality meshed well. Kim's only regret is that it took him so long to break the ice.

Divorce support expert Pat Gaudette tells the story of Maria, who, six months after her divorce, was drawn to Frank. Looking back, she has no idea why. They had nothing in common and no friends to share, but for some reason she was virtually obsessed with him. Luckily, a few months later she knew the relationship was a mistake, realizing it was based on short-term emotional needs—not the basis for a long-term commitment.

Unfortunately, many people make the same mistake. They fall in love with the first person who gives them comfort, and rush into a second or third marriage. And then the marriage ends after a few years or even months. With such a bad track record in our society for long-term relationships, some experts feel that pre-marital counseling should be a legal requirement for marriage.

## DON'T FORGET: MEN ARE NOT WOMEN

According to John Gray, author of *Men are from Mars, Women are from Venus,* men are socialized to give more in material, physical ways. And women are socialized to give more emotionally. Did you know that there is a lot going on in our mutual attraction that is unconscious? Relationship training makes us aware of our needs. It teaches us to pay attention to those needs and to how to make changes in our behavior to make the relationship work—

all ingredients for a more trusting friendship or marriage.

Even those without a partner can benefit from counseling. Divorced for six years, Kelly James, a 49-year-old engineer, compares her search for a companion to "a journey." After 17 years of marriage, she felt an intense pressure to immediately find someone new.

"My world as I knew it was erased," she says quietly. "I had to find a new job, a new place to live—and I had to learn to live without my children. When I first came out of my marriage, I was looking for something right away to fill the void."

Slowly, with the help of group therapy and by attending seminars and discussion groups, she was able to share her feelings and realize her completeness as a person, with or without a companion. "It's a sign of health," Ms. James adds.

## BAGGAGE

Are you wondering what the greatest turn-off is in dating? Baggage. *Don't bring your baggage to the table!* Every divorce has its own baggage. We're all angry about something. And rightly so. But others don't want to hear about it. After all, they have their own problems. Does your anger show up in everyday conversation? Is custody still an unresolved issue? Are you paying child support and alimony? If you don't have custody of your children, are you able to see them regularly? Then you still have some unreconciled issues that need to be dealt with *pronto!* Separating these issues or "garbage" may take awhile, but it's time well spent. During this period, try dating casually, without commitment. You need a break from pressure or added responsibility while you put your life back together.

## NET DATING

Meg Ryan and Tom Hanks did it in the movie *You've Got Mail,* so why can't you? They found love on the Internet, but, hey, just like dating, it has to happen naturally. Usenet news groups in the "rec" and "alt" hierarchies seem popular, such as groups where there are friendly people chatting. After meeting on the net and exchanging e-mails and messages for several months, you may try calling each other. If that's successful, then you may arrange to meet face to face. If you're an adventurer, here are some pros and cons to net dating:

- The Internet allows people to communicate over long distances at a low price. It even allows people to communicate all over the world easily.
- Internet relationships allow people to know each other without basing their likes or dislikes on superficial things—you're not judged by physical appearances.
- You're able to communicate more freely if you don't have to look at people face to face.
- *But* it's easy for people to lie to you if they don't have to look into your eyes.
- Long-distance relationships are hard and expensive to maintain. Plus, it's hard to get to know someone when they don't live near you, and you're unable to see them on a day-to-day basis.

## ARE YOUR KIDS READY?

If you have children, you must first consider their needs. With all the changes in your life, like dealing with your divorce or loss, a new job, a new home, and new friends, chances are your children have been neglected, even though they are the very people you are trying to protect.

Before bringing anyone new into their lives, spend some "alone time" with each child. Plan 15 minutes a day one-on-one with each child at bath time, story time, carpooling, walking the dog, or while playing in the sand pile. If you get on the floor with your child and enter into their make-believe world, then you can truly connect. It doesn't take much time. In fact, it may not be more than 15 minutes, but that time allows you to enter their world. Through creative play, you can find out how their day went, who their playmates are, and which teacher they like the most and why. Many psychologists use this technique. It's called play therapy, and it provides a natural setting where children relax and open up. Try it. It may save you time and allow you to reach your children in an honest, open way.

## CHAPTER 8 REVIEW: DATING AGAIN AND FINDING THE PATH TO HAPPINESS

- **Are your kids ready?** In order to assure they are ready for a change, spend extra time with them. Plan 15 minutes a day one-on-one with each child. Sit on the floor and join them in block building or playing with dolls. Take them to the park. Dig in the sand pile. It's amazing what you'll learn about them if you really listen with no interruptions.

- **Do you need extra help?** While going through a divorce or settling your husband's estate, you may be consumed by a new job, new home, new neighborhood, and mounting financial demands. During this tumultuous time, don't be afraid to ask for help from family or friends. When they say, "What can I do?" don't turn them down. Have a number of things already planned.

- **Involve the father.** Continue involving your children's father in the parenting process. Don't be afraid to ask him to help on the weekends; or if your child has a fever, don't be afraid to ask him to get the medicine at the drugstore. Whatever you do, don't criticize his efforts!

- **Pay attention to yourself.** Meditate. Plant a garden. Paint a picture. Go on a nature hike. Read your favorite book. Take precious time for yourself.

- **Put yourself out there.** Are you ready for romance? Then join a senior citizen center or a political cause, or volunteer for the art fair. Pick a project or class that you enjoy, not one just to meet men. You'll be surprised how easy it is, if you're natural and relaxed. Don't be afraid to go it alone. You'll meet lots of new friends.

- **Hold out for Mr. Right?** Forget about finding Mr. Right. He's not out there. Just date for fun.

Try to find a friend, not a lover. It puts you both more at ease. And don't limit yourself to one person. Enjoy, enjoy!

- **Don't get intimate too soon!** It rushes the relationship, as well as putting too much pressure on the guy to make a commitment. Remember, you do not need to be pressured, you've just endured a loss. Keep the dating light.

- **Watch for red flags.** Watch out for men who are possessive, short-tempered, critical of you, or have poor relations with their own parents or children. They may bring bad baggage into your relationship.

- **Protect yourself.** When you've found someone you trust and you want to be intimate, *wait!* Get an AIDS test. Wear condoms. Remember, sex is more than thrilling, it can kill you.

- **Give yourself the gift of time.** Dating is more enjoyable when you're not riding an emotional roller-coaster. Give yourself time to heal before falling for someone else.

# Chapter Nine

# solo
# parenting

There's no such thing as a "good divorce." Like an angry spider, divorce spins an ugly web around all those we treasure, trapping our minds, hearts, souls, and our most precious possession, our children.

Unfortunately, this web is invisible. Like tentacles, the silky threads slowly wrap around us, until they become suffocating. Each thread represents the emotions churning inside us. Anger, pain, despair, hurt, fear, longing, and anguish engulf us, refusing to let go.

## WHAT TO DO

When you are caught in this web, there are ways to cut the threads and escape, to maintain your sanity, and to hold your family intact.

But let's ease into this.

The best way to survive this difficult time is to *take care of yourself*. As my mother once said about rearing six children, "Honey, start out the way you want to end up."

This also applies to divorce. Show respect for yourself,

and it will be easier to manage this crisis. Surround your-self with support from friends, relatives, and neighbors who will listen to you and look out for you and your loved ones. As you gather these people around you, *don't be afraid to ask for help.* Don't be a superwoman. Don't try to be brave. Don't be shy. Up to 50 percent of marriages end in divorce, so you're not alone. But you won't make it without help.

It's also important to *think of yourself.* Evelyn's pedia-trician urged her to get a babysitter once a week so she could spend some time away from her 5-year-old, sug-gesting that after bedtime, her daughter didn't necessarily need her. Although reluctant, Evelyn, 38, soon joined a folk-dancing club which provided her with exercise and a social outlet. "After spending years only taking care of my child and going to work, I needed the chance to be with adults," Evelyn says. "It became my one night out—al-lowing me to return more refreshed and focused."

Whether it's a night spent at the theater or concert, or a quiet evening at home with your favorite book, it's im-portant to spend quality time with yourself. Deep breath-ing, meditation, bubble baths, or reading a racy novel may seem frivolous, but they allow us to spend time with our-selves, winding down from the stress of the week.

## SURVIVAL GROUPS GIVE SUPPORT

Since you're stuck being both mom and dad, you need other adults to share your questions or concerns. This will help you normalize your situation. You can find support groups through your church, parenting centers, divorce recovery groups, or your child's school.

Because divorce leaves us feeling emotionally vulnerable, our tendency is to focus on all the things we can't change versus what we can change. Christina McGhee, a marriage and family counselor, says, "As a parent you significantly impact your children's adjustment by:

- Maintaining a meaningful relationship with them.
- Providing them with a strong sense of family.
- Being a good listener and an approachable parent.
- Protecting them from conflict between you and your ex-spouse.
- Remaining an active and positive influence in your children's lives."

She created the web site divorceandchildren.com to make information and resources available for suddenly single parents.

## HOW DO WE START?

Ms. McGhee advises that we tell our children that the divorce is not their fault. Psychologist Bruce Drobeck agrees. He urges parents to reassure their children that they're in no way responsible for the breakup. They need to know that their parents still love them. And they need to have these questions answered: Will I be able to go to the same school? Will I be able to live in the same house? Will my friends still like me? Although children may not show it at first, divorce is disruptive to the child's whole routine and equilibrium.

## DANCE OF DEATH

Death is no different. It also leaves us entangled in an emotional web. Lisa Dickens, age 7, is an example of how grief can disrupt a person's world.

On a steamy day in August, a family of three slowly drove a boat through the crystal waters of Lake Texoma on the Texas–Oklahoma border. The father steered the boat with his 6-year-old daughter in his lap. The mother sat nearby. Suddenly, a wave swamped the boat, knocking the man into the water. In the confusion, the boat swerved. Quickly, the child took the wheel and maneuvered the boat in the direction of where her father's hat was floating in the water.

That was the last time the mother and daughter saw the father alive. Two days later, the authorities found him. He had been caught in the propellers and drowned.

The child, Lisa Dickens, spent one year refusing to talk about the accident. It wasn't until she received therapy from a children's grief counseling center that she was able to cope with her father's death.

Unfortunately, children are often neglected in the grieving process, grief expert Jane Le Vieux explains. "As an adult, you have probably experienced your own grief. When you were worried or bothered, you told someone who really cared and understood and you felt better. Unfortunately, children are not comforted in the same way. Often they are told, 'Don't bother your mother or father during this difficult time' or, 'Be strong and take care of your brother or sister.'"

Anna shares a similar story. Her father died of cancer

in February 1992. Afterward, Anna refused to discuss the incident. She began fighting with her two brothers. And one day, she covered the wall in angry scribbles with crayons—because, as her mother later discovered in therapy, Anna was angry at the "lumps in her daddy."

Helen Fitzgerald, author of *The Grieving Child* (Simon and Schuster, 1992), agrees. "Children react differently to death than do adults. These differences depend on their ages, the circumstances of the death, and the relationship to the deceased."

She urges parents to allow children to show their grief. Use correct language when talking to the child about death. Avoid phrases like "we have lost him" or "he is walking in the valley of the shadows." Euphemisms such as "he is sleeping," confuse the child. She also points out that, because adults and children react differently, "An adult may grieve intensely for two to three weeks, while a child might cry for ten minutes, then run off to play."

When someone we love dies, adds Fitzgerald, parents may be so uncomfortable that they exclude their children from most or all of the events associated with the death, providing them with little information about what is happening.

"In the mistaken belief that we are protecting our children," Fitzgerald says, "we deprive ourselves and our children of one of life's great opportunities for bonding: the sharing of a deeply felt, painful, and sad experience."

Whether because of divorce or death, the biggest adjustment in solo parenting is the fact that children are hit by so many emotions at once ... anger, bewilderment, fear of taking care of themselves. It's a major adjustment in their lives.

When dealing with divorce or death, you can't avoid the grief. And it has a way of sneaking up on you. You find yourself floundering, unable to concentrate on work. Unable to focus on your children. It's a very painful time.

At this time, you need lots of support, a circle of friends who accept you the way you are. Anytime you lose someone, it's not just about grief. It's also a loss of place. You may sell your home and move, or change schools or neighborhoods. There is a breakdown of family—a loss of a dream or ideal—where you find yourself asking: "Should I still celebrate my 25th anniversary? How long will my life be interrupted this way? How will I support my family?"

Because of the breakdown of finances, you are not just dealing with the loss of a husband and your children's father, you're dealing with the loss of a lifestyle. If there are distinct socioeconomic changes, if the kids must move or change schools, it's much more traumatic. Unfortunately, in the case of divorce, this is more common.

"If a person is living in a nice house, and then they have to move, that's a huge change," says Michael Smith, a psychologist. "They don't know new people, they don't feel safe."

When it comes to finances, let your children know that things will be a little tighter but *don't give them any details.* Don't discuss money and get emotional. That will needlessly frighten your children.

**DID YOU KNOW?**

- The U.S. Census Bureau reports that the average marriage in the United States lasts only seven years.
- Two-thirds of all women with children spend at least part of their lifetimes as single mothers.

## WHAT ABOUT LIVE-INS?

When Laura called her best friend at 3 o'clock in the afternoon, a man answered. When she asked to speak to her friend, the man quickly handed the phone to the 12-year-old daughter, who explained to the caller, "That's my mom's boyfriend. He lives here now."

Live-ins are not a good idea for children. The difficulty is that there's no guarantee the person will be there the next week. Or the next day. It's best if the parent takes care of his or her dating or sexual needs privately and does not involve the children prematurely.

After a divorce or death, there's a tremendous amount of emotional work that needs to be done. Rather than running off to find someone else to fill your emotional needs, put time into therapy. Get into a support group and get grounded.

**Vivian, 42.** The first year after her divorce, Vivian was a dishrag. She couldn't stop crying. The changes were too much. Forced to put her child in daycare, she cried on the way to the center, then cried on the way to work. "I placed my child in a daycare center located near a busy street. The house was old. But I had no choice. There were few qualified daycare centers in my small home town," says Vivian. "It was in an old house with space heaters. I worried about my child every minute of the day. I worried about her safety. I worried about her burning to death."

As the weeks passed, Vivian slowly regained confidence. After taking a job as a bank teller, she then moved to another newer bank, where she became an executive officer within a few months.

In addition to her career, Vivan also changed her attitude about parenting. "I spent the first year rushing home and cooking a scrumptious meal for my 3-year-old. Then I'd scream at her if she didn't eat it all. After a while, I realized that I needed to enjoy my time with her rather than feeling guilty for the time I was away."

The following summer, Vivian picked up her child one evening, then fed her a hot dog and went swimming in the apartment pool. "We had more fun that night, and I realized that my time with her was precious. I needed to relax and forget about being perfect."

You may find yourself frantically trying to get your life in order. It may take a year or two to readjust your lifestyle. The process can't be rushed. But there are positive ways to cut through the chaos.

## YOUR MISSION: DARE TO DISCIPLINE

According to child care experts, children need a foundation, a set of principles to guide them. So writing a mission statement, setting forth your family's goals and expectations, is a good place to start. It's also suggested that you have "family meetings" weekly. At these meetings schedules should be coordinated and problems addressed. Have your mission statement ready before you begin meeting.

Remember, a parent should be a role model. In meetings and during the week, avoid name-calling and physical punishment, and try to emphasize what your child does right rather than what he does wrong.

**EXAMPLE OF A MISSION STATEMENT**

"The [insert name of your family] family provides an environment where people treat each other fairly and with respect. Where people are loving to each other. Where people listen before they react. Where people don't accuse others or make accusatory, blanket statements like 'You always, you never.'"

## CARING FOR YOURSELF

Don't forget to set aside time for yourself. If you can get a neighbor to take your children for a pizza one afternoon, while you go to lunch with a friend, then your whole week will run easier. Or, the day your ex takes the children, go window shopping or go see your favorite movie. Avoid spending free time running errands or doing housework. Taking time for yourself allows you to be a better mother and worker.

## REFRAIN FROM CRITICIZING YOUR EX

If you criticize your ex, your children will know you are not trustworthy. Experts warn us about the difficulty of letting go in a divorce. "We often find ourselves legally divorced," says Dr. Drobeck, an adjunct professor at the University of North Texas, "but not psychologically divorced. The longer you allow your ex to push your buttons, the more power he has over you."

According to Joy Johnson, co-director of the Centering Group, based in Omaha, Nebraska, your children have a right to have both parents active in their lives. If you're mad at your ex because he hasn't paid child support, don't use the child to get back at him. Don't let your anger prevent your child from seeing her dad, or going to a concert with him.

In other words, avoid using your children as weapons against your ex. They have the right to be free of adult decisions, as well as the emotional baggage of mom and dad, says Christina McGhee, adult information and parental conflict consultant.

"If you have children," Dr. Drobeck adds, "divorce is like a living death, because a woman continues to be connected to her ex through her children. There will be a continuation of a relationship."

## HELPING KIDS COPE

Sometimes the initial change brought on by divorce pushes us over the edge—or almost.

**Chris, 40, with two children.** When she moved her children (Hank, 11, and Judy, 9) from their large country home to a small apartment in the city, her son began to get into fights at school. Labeled "the apartment kids," Hank and his sister were picked on by their wealthier schoolmates.

Chris tried everything to solve the problem. She appealed to school counselors and the principal. She invited friends over to play. She even signed her son up for football.

But it was never enough. The school was focused on sports, and when Hank, who was a natural athlete, was also chosen to join the baseball team, Chris had to turn it down. "It was too expensive," she said. "I couldn't afford to purchase the football and the baseball uniforms in the same year." When she withdrew her son from the team, she received angry calls from parents. Then the name-calling started. Hank grew anxious and aloof. And soon he was coming home with bruises and a bloody nose.

Although Hank received counseling, his grades began to fall, and he was forced to repeat the fifth grade.

**Katherine, 20.** As mentioned in Chapter 1, Katherine is another example of a child whose life is turned upside down by the loss of a parent. At the age of 20, Katherine was the last person to see her father alive. After taking her to dinner, he delivered her to her college dorm and kissed her goodbye. That evening, he returned to his hotel and took an overdose of insulin. A diabetic, he gave himself injections daily, but never a deadly dose. He wrote 10 suicide notes, one to his daughter saying that he was "sorry to have ruined her life."

Although Katherine remained at college, she quickly began to crumble. In three months she dropped 30 pounds and became bulimic. When she was arrested for shoplifting laxatives, her mother discovered that Katherine blamed herself for her father's suicide. "If only I would've realized how sick he was, I could've done something," she lamented.

When children and parents move through grief issues, they may "act in" or "act out," experts say. They may get extremely anxious or depressed, or they may acquire physical symptoms like headaches, sleep disturbance, or loss of appetite. If something is not done to address these issues, the grief can consume the child.

With some children, you may see their grades dropping, misbehavior in school, or fighting. Like Hank, they may appear angry, irritable, or more impulsive.

Depression is expressed differently in children. They may get more agitated, or become quiet and sad. It's difficult to predict which way they'll go. But you'll see a general disruption and their routine will be disturbed. Be aware of changes in your child's behavior and seek counseling when necessary.

## GET BACK ON TRACK

Since the divorce or death, you've found that you have half a paycheck. The college funds have disappeared into divorce fees. You've lost your housekeeper. The yard-man's gone (your husband always mowed the lawn). And your children have lost a father, a coach, a counselor, and in some cases, their best "buddy."

However chaotic your former life was, the loss has brought disaster upon your home. But this feeling of chaos is not permanent. Here are four ways to alleviate the mess in your life.

**FIRST, GET ORGANIZED.** If you can't figure a way out of the mess in your home, get an organized friend to help. Or hire your child's Montessori teacher. In a period of three hours, you'd be surprised how much neater your home will become.

**SECOND, MAKE A SCHEDULE.** Getting dressed. Showering. Eating breakfast. Brushing teeth. Combing hair. These rituals can be sources of tension, where parent and child are pitted against each other. And there is rarely a winner.

Mary Ann Little, a clinical psychologist and mother of three, has used her experiences when dealing with day-to-day parent–child conflicts to develop a set of learning tools called the Competent Kids Series, a group of parent handbooks and charts, published by Three Bears Books.

Dr. Little says that whether your child is age 2 or an adolescent, she needs order in the home. Your child needs a consistent schedule involving getting up and going to bed at the same times every day, going to school at the same time, and eating a healthy breakfast or dinner at the same time each morning or evening. Homework should be completed by a certain hour. And television should be banned until all homework is completed.

**THIRD, PUT BELONGINGS WHERE THEY BELONG.** In order to relieve mad chaos in the morning, each child should place jackets, soccer ball, or book bags at the back door in the evening. All papers should be signed and placed in book bags too.

FOURTH, START AN ACTIVITIES LIST. A record of all activities, including pick-up times, athletic events, tournaments, dance recitals, or theater classes should be placed on the refrigerator where everyone can read it.

In the process of a divorce or death, your family schedule may be wrecked. But the sooner that you put it back in action, the less harried the family will be.

Dr. Little, author of *Loving Your Children Better: Matching Parenting Styles to the Age and Stage of Your Children* (Westport Publishers, 1990), advises parents to be realistic when setting goals for their children. "If you have never asked your 7-year-old child to make a bed before, it's unreasonable to come to him and demand he make the bed by himself."

All chores, says Dr. Little should be introduced in steps. "Children learn by watching and helping an adult. They learn by practicing bigger tasks. And they learn by performing chores independently."

## FAMILY COUNSELING

When you're recuperating from a death or divorce, your emotions are intense. The children may be dealing with a new home, a different environment, a different school, and new friends. Plus, depending on the custody arrangement, they are missing their daddy tucking them in at night, or attending their basketball game or school performance.

In order to deal with these changes, experts recom-

mend family counseling *for all those involved.* Call in everyone in the divorced or separated families. If it's a death,
do the same thing. Family does not mean only immediate
family. It may include step-parents or step-siblings. Bringing in all family members allows you to get the whole
truth. And it enables a counselor to set up the *same rules
for everyone.*

In divorce, separated parents are forced to communicate through their kids, so they often get only half the
truth. In counseling, everyone's there together. You can
discuss certain issues and agree on specific rules pertaining to dating, curfews, homework, discipline, and so forth.


## TUG-OF-WAR

Is your 15-year-old trying to manipulate you? If mom
has custody, a teen may threaten to live with dad. Whoever is the most lenient parent is usually the one the teen
prefers to live with. If you're having this problem, it may
be a good idea to let your child move in with your spouse
(unless there is a problem with neglect or abuse). "Call
their bluff," experts say. "After all, your child may be fan-
tasizing about how easy dad is—when he lives there full
time, there may be a difference."

**Kate's story: raising a daughter alone.** Lively,
opinionated, and athletic, Kate, 47, who plays softball for
three different teams, seems like she's got everything
under control. But as she tells of the twelve-odd years
raising her daughter, alone, her enthusiasm sometimes
wavers.

"I was divorced at 35, and I was terribly immature,"

she says. "At the time, my daughter Loren was 8 years old, but she had a wisdom beyond her years." During this time, it sometimes felt like "Loren raised me . . . we grew up together," Kate says. "I'll admit, I let my daughter put pressure on me, because she didn't have two parents."

Although Kate had a master's degree in social work, she went into sales so she could earn more money. As a single mother, she was totally accessible to her daughter's needs. She worked hard to send her to parochial school, and then later to a private college. She served as den mother, carpooled her to basketball games and track meets, and baked cookies for her cheerleader squad. But, at times, it was not enough.

"As a single mother, I was totally accessible to my daughter's needs. I couldn't say, 'Go ask your father'—it was always me," Kate admits.

Kate did not remarry until her daughter graduated from college. "I didn't want to share Loren's upbringing with another person. I didn't trust anyone else to raise her."

## AVOID BEING A BUDDY

If you're not involved with other adults, your child sometimes fills the gap. As you share your fears about whether or not you're going to make your mortgage payment or lose your job, you're stripping a child of her childhood. This is information a child of any age cannot comprehend. Even if your child is mature, it is inappropriate to force her to listen to adult problems. Without an adult in the house, it's easy to fall into this trap, and it puts your child in an untenable situation. It's not the child's responsibility to become the caretaker. *That's your job*. Experts warn that sharing the intimate details of your life is also inappropriate. Don't discuss how much money you do or do not make. Don't report what the attorney said during court. And don't describe why your boyfriend is sexy. A young child (or even a teenager) doesn't need to hear "adult talk." Their world is already topsy-turvy.

They need to be protected and surrounded by *normalcy*. They need to know that the models in their lives are stable and secure. Even if you are not secure during this time of loss, you need to assure your children that although this is a rocky time, everything will turn out okay.

Divorce or death hits us like a ton of bricks. Even if we expect the loss, it always comes as a shock. Like a tornado, our emotions assault us. Pain, anger, fear, despair, and longing engulf us. Not all at once. Sometimes the emotions continue for years. And during this time, we're expected to be the best of parents. Sometimes, this seems like too much to ask.

Children are intuitive. They can tell if we care, if we're there for them. Through this process, you and your child may become enemies. Or partners. Sometimes too-close partners. Sometimes healthy partners. But, as you gain your independence, a sense of balance will occur. You'll work through your emotions and become a "grown-up" again. And then, you and your child will learn about living and loving, and you'll rejoice in the journey.

## CHAPTER 9 REVIEW: TURN SOLO PARENTING INTO A HAPPY TRIP

- **Take care of yourself as well as the kids.** Show respect for yourself. Walk, jog, do yoga, meditate. Take time for long, hot baths and adult conversation.
- **Don't be afraid to ask for help.** Always have a back-up plan, using neighbors, relatives, or friends. Don't try to be a supermom!
- **Seek support from groups.** Sharing your story with others helps normalize your situation. After you've received support and learned what you can change, only then can you begin to help your children.
- **Reassure your children.** Remind them that they are not responsible for the divorce or the death of your spouse.
- **Answer questions.** Answer questions about changes in your children's lives honestly, but respond positively. "Yes, you may have to change schools. But look at it as an adventure, where you'll meet new people, do new things."
- **Describing death.** Use the correct language when describing death. Phrases like "he passed away" are confusing to young children.
- **Do not exclude your children.** Let them in on events associated with death, like the funeral or wake. Let them share the death experience. Don't say to your child, "You need to be a big boy and not cry." This prevents him from expressing his grief.

- **Don't dump.** Work through your own emotions. Avoid dumping them on your child.
- **Dare to discipline.** Create a family mission statement listing goals and expectations. Meet once a week in a family meeting and address these goals.

# from the voices of famous women . . . inspiring advice

Through interviews with six famous women in various fields, from entertainment to medicine to politics, come six unique perspectives in each woman's own voice, as to how each has handled loss. You'll meet:

Ann Richards, divorced, outspoken former governor of Texas

Joan Rivers, widowed comedian, actress, radio talk-show host, and entrepreneur

Dr. Nancy Snyderman, divorced medical correspondent for *ABC News*

Liz Carpenter, widowed veteran Washington insider and journalist

Beverly Garland, widowed actress who starred in the popular television series *My Three Sons*.

Kitty Carlisle Hart, widowed game show host, singer, and indefatigable promoter of the arts

These women may move in different circles, but they all have a common bond. They've each lost a partner, either through divorce or death. Their experiences prove that there is a difference between loneliness and living alone. From these women, you'll learn how to reinvent yourself, discover secret passions, nurture new friendships, and live life again.

You'll also find that these women may not be as different from you as you thought. They've all struggled in their lives, adapting to one crisis after another. They've all made serious mistakes, over and over again, before changing their lives. Some lost their family, friends, finances, and self-respect. But after suffering a loss, all of them learned one thing: to get up and get going again—to come out of hiding and get on with life.

Take Dr. Nancy Snyderman, for example. After making poor choices in relationships for years, she decided to remain single, relishing her time alone with her young daughters and giving herself time to grow. In her book *Necessary Journeys* she describes her plight. "The solitary path I'd chosen taught me a great deal about the importance and meaning of relationships in my life. I'd always looked toward the relationship I had with a man as the primary source of my definition as a woman. Now, without a man in my life, I had to look elsewhere for meaning and connection."

Ann Richards has a different story.

After losing the governor's race to George W. Bush, she left politics and, with few savings, pursued another career. Today, among other endeavors, she lectures on health and fitness throughout the country, consulting with large corporations. And she plans to remain single. "I wouldn't have it any other way," she says. "It's a great time of my life. A time of joy and freedom."

Whether you remain single for a lifetime, or remarry, these high-profile women will help teach you to discover your inner spirit.

## ANN RICHARDS

*"I don't own anything I have to feed or water. When I leave my condo, I can walk out and lock the door. I can be gone for 20 minutes or 20 years, and nothing inside will suffer."*

Ann Richards was born on September 1, 1933, in a farming community in Lakeview, Texas. The only child of Cecil and Iona Willis, she never lacked for attention. At an early age, her father taught her to hunt and fish, and her mother provided piano and elocution lessons.

The elocution lessons paid off.

While attending Baylor University in Waco, Texas, she became known as a fierce intercollegiate debater, paving her own way to a career in politics.

Years later, in 1976, Ann was elected the first female county commissioner of Travis County. In 1983 she became state treasurer, and in 1990, at the age of 57, she won the race for governor.

But that was only the beginning. Now, at age 66, Ann is a shining example of an independent woman.

---

After almost 30 years of marriage, Ann Richards divorced and met the challenge of living alone head-on.

"The initial trauma of being alone is difficult because you assume that you are going to live the rest of your life with someone," Ann says. "And I suppose that none of us feels that our own company is good enough for a lifetime. Yet, in reality, the most important person to learn to live with is ourselves. We invest so much time in the comfort of others that we often ignore the nurturing we need for ourselves."

Ann Richards is an independent role model for women. She was born during the Depression in an impoverished farm community in Texas, an only child. As "daddy's girl," her father taught her to be a crack shot, regularly taking her deer- and bird-hunting. When speaking about her childhood, she says, "I can't remember walking; I ran everywhere. I climbed trees. When *Superwoman* comics came out, I got on the roof of the garage with a rope and jumped off." She grew up intelligent, witty, and full of energy. And she used these qualities in her political career years later.

Appearing as the keynote speaker at the Democratic National Convention in 1988, she turned into a national celebrity with her famous comment: "Poor George. He can't help it. He was born with a silver foot in his mouth."

Two years later she ran for governor of Texas, successfully beating Clayton Williams. During her administration, Texas prospered. When her term ended, the budget was balanced for the first time in many years.

But Ann Richards' private life was difficult. Before she ran for state treasurer, her family held an intervention session, encouraging Ann to enter an alcoholic treatment center.

When Ann returned from treatment, she was a new person. "I don't think I could have made the race without going through the [alcohol] treatment," she says in *The Thorny Road to Texas* by Mike Shropshire and Frank Schaefer. "It wasn't like going somewhere and not drinking. You go through all the periods of your life in that thirty days. It's pretty dramatic. You spend all that time assessing what really matters. The feelings you have are entirely positive, because you have met yourself and accepted yourself. Few people have that chance. It's a tremendous luxury—a rebirth."

In spite of her success, she and her husband separated and later divorced.

"I think my relationship with David, which had been so totally intense, underwent a dramatic change. We had been so totally bound to each other that [my getting into politics] was very difficult for him," she told the *Dallas Morning News*.

"Getting a divorce was the hardest thing I've ever done. Harder than alcoholism, harder than treatment, harder than politics," she says in Shropshire and Schaefer's book. Later, she admitted, "I thought I would die if I were not married to David Richards."

But Ann Richards didn't die. She got on with her life, and some years later, on November 8, 1990, she became the 46th governor of Texas. At the end of her term, a no-new-taxes budget was passed for 1993. After losing the governor's race to George W. Bush in 1994, she did not look back. "When I left the governor's office, I virtually had no money at all. You can't make money in public office. That's an expensive proposition," she says.

"I worked hard to establish new sources of income, and I did it joyously. I'm having a wonderful time. One of my life goals is to learn new things. I can't stand to do what I've always done."

Just as in politics, she jumped in and got to work, making television commercials, lecturing, and serving on the boards of top corporations throughout the nation.

"I love being single," she says with a lilt in her voice. She objects to using the word "survive" when referring to being single. "It makes me think that I'm fighting against adversity, like I'm trying to keep from drowning. I don't like to think of being single that way."

"I love my life now," she continues. "I can't imagine it any other way. I have the comfort of a close relationship with a man [sportswriter Bud Shrake] I've been with for 15 years, but neither of us would choose the life of living with another person again. We value our space. Our individuality. Our opportunity to choose where we want to go. And what we want to do. Living alone offers that."

When you listen to Ann Richards talk, you realize she's a fountain of knowledge on how to handle living alone and being the better for it. Here are some things she said:

*Handling Depression.* "One of my favorite sayings is, 'If

I'm in a bad mood, I change my mind.' If you want to be in control of your life, be in control of what you think."

*Don't Let Others Make You Feel Guilty.* She suggests working hard at rejecting old tapes which program your mind, like "If you divorce, you're throwing good years down the drain," "Gee, you must be lonely," or "I'm afraid the children will suffer." When people tell you these things, they are often imposing thoughts of how their life would be if they were in your circumstance.

*Avoid Being Dependent on Others.* "I think that women who set themselves up in a dependent posture, either on their children, their spouse, their significant other, or whoever it is, are making a mistake. If you're depending on others for your well-being, you are setting yourself up for disappointment. Because no one person can possibly meet all your needs. Only you can do that."

*Getting Over Your Grief.* "Get up and get out of the house!" she exclaims. "Get rid of all that *stuff.* Sell whatever you're living in and move to a small space. Avoid having an extra bedroom where someone can come and sleep in your house."

*Creating Boundaries.* "I've established life on my own terms. I've had to draw my own boundaries. I don't ask anyone's permission." Also, she doesn't do a traditional Christmas—"I don't put up a tree anymore, and I don't own an ornament." Instead, she travels with her children each holiday, visiting places like Jamaica or Europe.

*Handling Grandchildren.* "I don't babysit. I'm the grandmother who buys the presents and writes the checks," she says laughing. She prefers to ask one of her seven grandchildren out to dinner, where she can get to know what's going on better—instead of entertaining the entire family as a group.

*Attitude.* "I've come to the period of my life when I can see the end of it. If I'm lucky, I've got 20 years left where I'm going to be physically and mentally able to do what I'd like to do. So, I better figure out how I'm going to spend those 20 years."

*Managing Money.* "You should never depend on another human being for your income. Financial security is the greatest security there is."

*Divorce.* Today, Ann Richards has this to say about her divorce: "I don't mourn that passing." She also notes, "The impact of divorce is enormous. But out of it there is a really positive side. I've never lived alone before, ever. To me, that's an enormous accomplishment."

### JOAN RIVERS

*"The worst time, I think, was when there was no work. I just couldn't make a living. And yes, my daughter and I weren't there together, and yes, my husband had committed suicide, and yes, everything was horrible— and I couldn't pay the bills! It was terrifying. As my agent had said, 'Nobody wants to see a woman whose husband has committed suicide.'"*

Born Joan Molinsky on June 8, 1933, in New York City, Joan Rivers, now 66, has never had a dull moment.

Comedian, author, director, actress, talk-show

host, and entrepreneur, Joan Rivers's roller-coaster career has been daunting at times.

Although her father was a doctor, Joan pursued comedy with little support from her parents. After leaving Barnard College she joined the comedy circuit, playing to coffee shops in Greenwich Village and small, seedy night clubs for seven years. Discovered by Johnny Carson, she began appearing regularly on the *Tonight Show,* and a star was born.

---

When brash, funny Joan Rivers gets serious, her comments are both poignant and wise. She's the first to admit that her life's like *"War and Peace,* heavy on the war," she says.

In 1986, after Fox's *The Late Show Starring Joan Rivers* was canceled, her husband of 22 years, Edgar Rosenberg, killed himself by taking an overdose of pills. Rivers was broke, nobody would hire her, and her daughter was barely speaking to her. But Rivers is a fighter, and she went on to create her *QVC* jewelry business, her Emmy Award–winning talk show *The Joan Rivers Show,* her relationship with *E! Entertainment Network,* and her current pride and joy: a radio talk show also called *The Joan Rivers Show.* Plus, there's her latest book, *From Mother to Daughter: Thoughts and Advice on Life, Love and Marriage* (Birch Lane, 1998).

In addition to her entertainment appearances, Joan also travels throughout the country speaking to women in transition, women who are dealing with loss through death or divorce.

In her book *Bouncing Back* (HarperCollins, 1997), Joan

writes about hitting bottom after the death of her husband. She says, "My husband of 22 years killed himself.
My career is over. I am a widow, and my daughter, the
most important person in my life, is now fatherless. Despite the fact that we live in a big house and have nice
things, we are, because of bad investments, nearly broke."

Joan also writes about making it back to the top. She
describes ways to recharge your life and bounce back from
your grief. She's particularly sensitive to women who are
coming out of a long relationship. And she understands
their pain, anxiety, and concerns.

After Edgar's death, Joan Rivers experienced a heart-
breaking estrangement from her daughter, Melissa, as
they sorted through their grief. As if that weren't bad
enough, she also found herself in financial ruin when
Joan Rivers Products, the jewelry company she started,
was forced into bankruptcy when the parent company,
Regal Communications, assumed a debt of $37 million.

Because of these losses, Joan Rivers was forced to reinvent her life, to start over again. Now, when she goes out
on the lecture circuit, she shares her story, encouraging
others to bounce back and reshape their lives.

When she gets up in front of an audience, she often
says, "There are many self-help books by Ph.D.'s, but I
hold a different degree: an I.B.T.I.A.—I've Been Through
It All. This degree comes not on parchment but gauze, and
it entitles me to tell you that there is a way to get through
*any* misfortune." Then, she laughs and jokes as she tells
how she bounced back. Her perky, positive attitude
demonstrates that it's true.

But bouncing back wasn't easy for Joan Rivers, especially after her husband took his life in a hotel in Pittsburgh while on a business trip. She and her daughter were consumed with guilt. Like many left behind by suicide, they asked, "What if I'd met him in Pittsburgh? What if I'd had one more day to talk him out of his depression?"

As her companion and business partner, her husband shared a unique bond with Joan. Unlike most Hollywood couples, they were devoted to each other. After 22 years of marriage, they loved the life they'd built together, as well as the life they'd built for their daughter, Melissa, a sophomore in college.

"I also missed Edgar on a very practical level. He wasn't only my best friend, lover, and partner, but he was the man who knew how to balance the checkbook, program the VCR, and park the car; I could do none of these things."

While dealing with the loss, Joan was forced to learn to do the very things she'd depended on her husband for. In order to prepare herself, she enrolled in a course at the University of California at Los Angeles called Accounting 101, and there she learned the basics for financial management.

While she was picking up the pieces of her life, Joan was also struggling to rebuild her career. Although her investors encouraged her to sell everything and retire, that was the last thing she wanted. Because no one would hire her, she was unemployed for the first time since 1968. "There is no prospect bleaker," she says in her book *Bouncing Back*. "A person must have a reason to get up in the morning, and now I had none: I was unemployed."

But it was more than unemployment. Joan had lost her audience, something vital to a performer.

Although Joan feels it's important to grieve, she believes in keeping it short. She suggests crawling under the covers for 48 hours, but no more than that. Like many widows, she found herself wandering from room to room, feeling empty and alone. But she didn't stay in this state. She joined friends for lunch and made an effort to get out of the house. When wallowing, she suggests you make a list of everything that makes you sad, writing down all the gripes, pains, and grudges you can think of. After the list grows long, she guarantees you'll laugh at the results and gladly throw it away!

Joan had a long list of items, not the least of which was her anger with her dead husband. He'd not only deserted her, but also his daughter. His suicide threw her into a rage. One day, she picked up his pills and threw them all over the bathroom, then she kicked the dresser, almost breaking her toe. "I missed Edgar and grieved for him, I was furious at him for willfully leaving me—and, much worse, his daughter," Joan stated in her book.

One way she dealt with her grief was by writing him a poison pen letter, filled with negative thoughts. She suggests this method to others suffering a loss, writing as fast as you can, getting it all out. Then, after you've finished, don't mail the letter—throw it away.

After almost two years of grieving, Joan and her daughter finally came to accept Edgar's death. They realized that he had planned to kill himself, and there was nothing they could do to stop him. It was then that their anger with each other dissipated. Their grief was beginning to be resolved.

When her investors told her to sell everything and retire, she refused. When well-meaning friends told her to stay put, and remain at home in Los Angeles, she decided to move to New York. Through this experience, she learned it's more important to listen to your inner voice than to listen to the advice of others. According to Joan, "One rule of survival is: Make your own rules. *The hell with what anyone thinks about the way you're acting; listen only to yourself.* And while listening, remember the words of Nietzsche: 'Whatever doesn't kill me makes me stronger.'"

With this in mind, Joan moved to New York City and started a new life. She renovated an apartment, while enjoying the excitement of the city. "Oh, to see real people! The joy of walking along Madison Avenue!" she exclaimed. Leaving the memories of her home opened her up to a new beginning. And she welcomed the pace of New York. She found herself walking in her neighborhood, joking with the doormen on the way. Exercise became a daily habit. She worked out on a treadmill an hour a day, plus, she didn't flinch from sprinting up the office building stairs on her way to an appointment. She also began asking a taxi driver to drop her off two blocks from her destination, so she could walk the rest of the way. Not only did exercise keep her busy, but the endorphins kept her from getting depressed, something she advises for others suffering from a loss.

If your situation allows it, Joan also had this final bit of advice. Get a dog, even it's a small dog, like a Chihuahua. They bark and they're great protection.

## NANCY L. SNYDERMAN, M.D.

*"Inside the white coat, I was somebody: Dr. Nancy Sny-derman. The white coat off, I was a self-conscious young woman who was failing at her marriage."*

Nancy Snyderman, 48, worked hard at keeping on track. The eldest daughter of a prominent doctor in Fort Wayne, Indiana, she always dreamed of entering the medical profession.

At 31, after completing medical school and her residency, she moved to Little Rock, Arkansas, to begin practicing as a surgeon. In addition to a demanding medical practice, Nancy began working part-time as the medical correspondent on ABC's *Good Morning America*.

Nancy is also the author of *Dr. Snyderman's Guide to Good Health: What Every Forty-Plus Woman Should Know About Her Changing Body* (William Morrow & Company, 1996), and *Necessary Journeys* (Hyperion, 2000).

For years, Dr. Nancy Snyderman, the medical correspondent for *ABC News*, has greeted us warmly with the perfect bedside manner. A surgeon, specializing in otolaryngology (which has to do with cochlear implants, pediatric hearing disorders, sinus and allergy conditions, head and neck surgery, and otology), she's won our trust reporting on the latest medical findings in children's vaccines, menopause, and heart disease. She's also interviewed Nobel laureates, Somali warlords, refugees from Bosnia, and soldiers during the Gulf War.

In spite of the major accomplishments in her career, Nancy Snyderman's personal life has not been easy. And, until recently, it's something she's been hesitant to talk about. In her book *Necessary Journeys* she admits, "I never expected life to be so messy."

Along with becoming a doctor and medical correspondent, she was married two times, went broke once, and started her life over alone, with two children, in a brand new city. All by the age of 36.

What caused her this inner turmoil? Rape. While sleeping in her college dorm one night, she was attacked at knifepoint. She was only 19. For years, she didn't tell a soul.

When asked why she didn't tell her parents, she says, "I haven't a clue. I don't have any explanation. All my life, I wanted to stay on track. I always wanted to stay the course." An admitted people-pleaser, Nancy feared disappointing the people she loved.

Whether from shock or shame, Nancy didn't speak of the rape for years. She buried it deep inside, affecting her future relationships with men. "Not telling was most unhealthy," she admits. "It affected my other decisions."

"I sought out men who were nice to me on the surface, who validated my chipped-away sense of self," she says in her book. "I cowered when they raised their voices, and I learned to distance myself emotionally whenever the going got rough. I could not permit them ever to be angry and, when they were, I drifted away in response."

She blamed this behavior on the rape. "The rape walled me off, but because I hadn't confronted what had happened to me, it cast a dark shadow," she said.

Although she had a strong persona outwardly, on the inside she was confused. After the incident, she gained 40 pounds and became self-conscious about her body.

At 24, she married a family friend, someone with whom she felt safe. But when she entered her surgical residency, the marriage fell apart. As her involvement in medicine escalated, her husband began to withdraw emotionally. "Nothing in my husband's childhood had prepared him for living with a wife who was in this kind of career."

After they divorced a few years later, Dr. Snyderman relocated to Little Rock, Arkansas. In no time, she managed to land two jobs: one as a surgeon, the other as a medical correspondent for ABC.

Onscreen, she created a demand for her reporting because of her caring attitude and her crisp, professional delivery. Although Nancy's career flourished, she was still struggling with discovering her inner self. "I still thought that the answer to my problems was finding a man," she admitted.

And then she met the man of her dreams. A handsome, well-established entrepreneur. "I was flattered that a man apparently as sophisticated and worldly as he was—he wore Turnbull & Asser shirts, drove a jazzy, black BMW, drank Diet Coke out of Waterford crystal, worked in exquisitely appointed surroundings—wanted me." Nancy thought his approval of her was a measure of her worth. Two months after their first date, they married, with her husband making all the arrangements. He hired the caterer, ordered the cake and flowers, and selected the church. "After working so hard at establishing my career as a surgeon, I was glad to turn over the responsibility to another. I turned over the reins."

Again, Nancy tended to define herself by the man she was with. She felt like a princess who'd been rescued by a knight in shining armor. Like many women, she was more interested in *what* her husband was, in terms of his achievements, than *who* he was.

Unfortunately, she came to regret this choice.

In the ensuing years, warnings began appearing in the relationship. When Nancy wanted to adopt a child, her husband resisted. Although she went on with the adoption, it was obvious that her husband was more interested in throwing lavish parties and, as her parents commented, "living beyond their means." But Nancy paid no attention. "Looking back, I see there was a whole lot I didn't pay attention to. I handed over my paychecks and he paid the mortgage and the bills, just the way my father handled the family finances when I was growing up."

Then, one day, Nancy's comfortable little world took an unsettling spin. She received a disturbing phone call from a man claiming that her husband was having an affair with his wife. In a panic, she called her mother, who advised her to look into their safety deposit box. When Nancy did, she discovered a hidden life led by her husband. There were overdue credit cards she hadn't known they had, irate letters from the IRS, and expensive purchases for women she'd never heard of.

Months after the divorce, Nancy was forced to sell her

home and immediately pay the IRS off with the proceeds. "It was the most humiliating day of my life," she says. "Although I made a six-figure income, I left that marriage with little more than the clothes on my back."

In 1988, she moved to San Francisco to begin a new life. At the time, her daughter was a toddler, and Nancy was pregnant with her second child. She recalls her first moments in San Francisco sitting in the apartment's empty space, waiting for her furniture to arrive from Little Rock. Her daughter was staying with her family in Indiana. And, as she describes in her book, she was "utterly, totally alone in this unfamiliar city that was supposed to be a place for new beginnings. Scrunched in a corner of the living room, feeling more like a lost child than anything else. I drew my knees to my chest and rocked and cried."

With time, though, Nancy healed. "There's nothing like thinking all has been taken away," she explains. "It gave me the resilience to know that I had to start over."

After taking a job in a local university hospital, she continued to work part-time as a medical correspondent for ABC, and for the first time in her life, Nancy accepted solitude. She faced the bumps in her life and began to recognize her own worth. "One of the best gifts I received was learning to redefine myself."

The move to San Francisco was life-saving for Nancy because there she could start over. After the birth of her baby, she came to know the difference between solitude and loneliness. Refusing to date, she learned that if you don't pause for introspection, you can't analyze your life. As she balanced her life between two jobs and her young children, Nancy began to appreciate herself. "I was working hard to become a good mom, putting my daughters in the center of my life, making my family a unit," she says.

Throughout these years, she discovered that *whatever* you are, a doctor, lawyer, or firefighter, is not as important as *who* you are. This realization gave Nancy the inner peace and confidence to enjoy her single status. "I'd spent two decades of my so-called adulthood thinking that I existed as a woman only by being a part of a couple," she says, noting that without a man in her life, she was forced to look elsewhere for meaning and connection.

In 1990, she met a man who would later become her loving husband, but she did not marry him for three years. She chose to remain single . . . at least for a while.

This new life, on her own with her children, helped her to discover who she was. And it allowed her to realize that a relationship with a man was not about caretaking but about partnership. "I relished living alone," she says pensively. After putting the kids to bed in the evening, she recalls gazing out the window at the twinkling city lights below. "At last, I loved the silence. I was able to live without an adult voice. It was freeing."

**LIZ CARPENTER**

*"Life has always led me to where things are happening, where people were exhilarating, where actions and laughter came quickly."*

Liz Carpenter, 80, has spent her life in politics. She helped found the National Women's Political Caucus, served as an assistant secretary in the Department of Education, and was a consultant to the LBJ Library. She served as Lady Bird Johnson's press secretary and chief of staff during the LBJ administration. As a speechwriter, she wrote one of Lyndon Johnson's famous speeches, delivered at Andrews Air Force Base after he stepped off the plane that carried the coffin of John F. Kennedy back to Washington. With her dear friend Erma Bombeck and colleagues Gloria Steinem, Betty Friedan, Bella Abzug, and Maureen Reagan, she also chaired a national organization that fought for passage of the Equal Rights Amendment.

In addition, Liz Carpenter writes for magazines and books. *Getting Better All the Time, Unplanned Parenthood, Confessions of a Seventy-Something Surrogate Mother,* and *Start With a Laugh* have made her popular on the lecture circuit.

---

Panache. A sense of style and bravado. The willingness to take risks. These are the qualities that author and lecturer Liz Carpenter possesses. She advises widows, "Build your own network. Let your home establish your identity. Don't wait for someone to offer you an invitation. You do the inviting."

Now, at 80, she has adapted to living alone, attributing her happiness to an upbeat attitude and a network of friends. She gets up at the crack of dawn and feeds the deer on her front lawn. While admiring the sunrise, she uses her time alone to write, speak, and entertain.

But it wasn't always so.

When Liz Carpenter's husband, Les, died of a heart attack, she was 54 years old. After 32 years, her partner in marriage and work was gone. As residents of Washington, D.C., she and Les, both journalists, reported on the political scene. They danced and dined with ambassadors and top politicians, and their lives were never dull.

Suddenly, with the death of her husband, Liz's life came to an abrupt halt. At the time, she thought her loneliness would continue forever. In her book *Getting Better All the Time* (Simon and Schuster, 1987), she says, "When you're suddenly alone, there is a terrible vacuum in your life. You wonder, will anyone ever love me?"

Like many widows, immediately following her husband's death Liz was forced to make another decision. With the Republicans taking over, she had to decide if it was time to make a change and return home to Texas.

But she had mixed feelings. "It was real anxiety deciding to relocate to Austin. I'd spent 34 years in politics. Would I miss the chatter of the galleries? Would I miss being in the know?"

She worried about changing lifestyles, but when her niece found a house high on a hill overlooking the skyline of Austin, Liz knew this was to be her new home.

And because of her creativity and spirit, home it became. "I used my home as a gathering place for interesting, creative minds," she explains, "and continued to work. I still earn my own living."

"Hostesses once thought their guest lists should include only couples, like Noah's Ark," she says. "Without my husband, there were no longer two of us, there was just me."

She began throwing parties, inviting old university friends, writers, professors, artists, actors, architects, and politicians. She also made it a point to mix the ages and occupations.

On Sundays she'd hold an afternoon salon, pulling out her wedding china and decorating with fresh-cut flowers. Then, she'd ask each guest to bring a covered dish and a poem that they'd written. "I'd ask writers in Austin— some I didn't know at all," she says. And through these gatherings, she widened her circle and her audience.

One night, when the moon was full, around a campfire at a nearby ranch the coyotes started howling in the river bottom. Her friends howled back, and within a few minutes, they saw the yellow eyes of the coyotes staring at them in the dark.

That was the beginning of the "Bay-at-the-Moon Club," which now meets once a month on the night of a full moon. In addition to baying at the moon, the group travels to entertain at holiday parties, senior centers, or other gatherings. Their group has become the toast of Austin. And this activity helped Liz emerge from her grief.

"Widows often take on a look of no laughter," adds Liz. "They wear a blue funk on their faces. You can spot them."

"Drop that heavy heart," she says. "Surround yourself with music and lighthearted friends. Keep funny books by your bed. Instead of lying there in misery, read."

"When you're single," she continues, "you have to be willing to take risks. You have to make your own stew. If you wait for invitations, you're going to be disappointed." She suggests making your single-woman house the center for others to gather, including in your circle of friends, people who make you laugh.

"As you work through your loss," she says, "be kind to yourself by getting a facial or a massage. And don't forget to do something ridiculous each week. The ability to shock your children is life-enhancing. It's essential."

## BEVERLY GARLAND

*"You have to hold your head up and face the world. Not give into this tremendous grief and shut yourself away. And as you do this, it becomes obvious that death is nothing. This person is still around you. If you talk to them, they're right there."*

Beverly Garland's television career kicked into high gear during the mid-sixties, when she starred in two high-profile series, *The Bing Crosby Show* (1964–1965) and *My Three Sons* (1969–1972), in which she played the wife of Fred MacMurray. Then, a new generation came to know Garland in her role as Kate Jackson's mom in the 1983–1987 hit *Scarecrow and Mrs. King*. In the '90s, she reappeared—as Teri Hatcher's mother on *Lois and Clark* (1994–1996). Today, she has a recurring role as a mental patient (which, she says, "I just love, it's so wild!") in the soap opera *Port Charles*.

In addition to acting, Ms. Garland, 71, is well-known as the glamorous owner of the Beverly Garland Holiday Inn in North Hollywood, where you'll often catch a glimpse of her on the grounds. The hotel is located just a few doors from Universal Studios.

---

Beverly Garland is not someone you can easily ignore. She's a gutsy gal, spinning hilarious tales one minute and being boldly honest the next. You'd never know she was a widow who recently lost her husband of 40 years.

When she first met her husband, Fillmore Crank, a successful developer and businessman, he was a widower with two children. After dating fast-talking men from Hollywood, she initially found him dull. "It took him forever to get a sentence out," she says chuckling. She found his dry sense of humor hard to understand—although on their second date, things changed. At a friend's party, he sat at one end of a long table, she on the other. When romantic music began playing, she looked at Fillmore, thinking he was something special. "It was just a feeling. But I went with it," she says. "I knew he adored me. He showed his feelings from the start."

And now, with his sudden death barely a year ago, she's trying hard to cope. Fillmore was diagnosed with primary liver cancer. Two weeks later he died.

"When I lost Fillmore, I lost a whole chunk of myself. I didn't know who I was," she says. "Half of me disappeared down the drain."

But keeping him in the moment of her life is the way she copes with her grief. "I talk to him a lot, and he talks to me. Sometimes I give him hell and he does the same," she says, laughing. When she received a ticket for parking in a handicapped spot, she heard her husband scolding her, "Beverly, you deserved that damn ticket!"

"I'll admit it. I'm still learning from him," she says, smiling.

But like many widows who suddenly lose their husbands, her journey has not always been easy. At one time, she covered her head with the sheets, refusing to leave her bed for 48 hours. But Fillmore kept talking to her, prodding her, encouraging her to continue her life. Getting up and leaving home was difficult, though, because she missed him terribly.

She missed his positive strokes, his feedback, his ability to keep her on track. During their marriage, he was never threatened by her successful career. He challenged her to do new things, like becoming a spokesperson for his hotel business. "Although I was an actress, the thought of getting up in front of people terrified me," she admits. As Beverly struggles with his loss, she hears Fillmore coaching her, encouraging her to survive. During this time she said to herself, "You have to be very strong. You must give yourself credit for being a viable, attractive woman who can live her life without this man. You have to hold your head up and face the world. Not give into this tremendous grief and shut yourself away. And as you do this, it becomes obvious that death is nothing. This person is still around you. If you talk to them, they're right there.

"I think that's what comforts me—I keep him in the moment of my life."

Like many women, when Beverly became a widow,

she was excluded from some couples' activities. But she understands that many people are uncomfortable with tragedy. "It's not easy having someone to dinner who has lost their spouse," she says.

Instead, Beverly suggests that women who have recently lost spouses seek out other widows who share the same loss. "Get out and meet people, find a support group," she says. Beverly tried going to an analyst, but she spent each session crying so badly, she couldn't talk about her husband. At that time, she stopped therapy, because she didn't know who she was, or where she was going. In spite of this emotionally bleak period, she discovered that time was her best friend, allowing a "new you to emerge each day."

"My job at the hotel is my lifeline," Beverly admits. "I don't think I could do it without it. It's become my mission." As owner and operator of the Beverly Garland Holiday Inn in North Hollywood, she and her son James oversee the day-to-day operation, including renovations and repairs. She rises at dawn, walks her dog in the hills above her home on Mullholland Drive, then drives to her office. As she works, she still hears Fillmore coaching her in business affairs. He encourages her to listen and avoid making snap decisions. "I watch things carefully here," she says. "We're cautious about our costs."

She advises other women in her situation to go out and find something they care about. Something they regard as a passion, whether it be a job, volunteer work, or a cause. "You gotta go out and do it," she says, emphatically. "Put one foot in front of another and do it. Don't flubber around, you've got to be strong. Make up your mind, get out there and try. It will save your life."

After Fillmore died, Beverly's children urged her to have an assistant move in and care for her, because they were afraid for her to be alone. "I wasn't about to do that," she says flatly. Beverly now spends her early morning hours paying her bills and answering her own fan mail. "I don't want anyone hanging over me, I don't need that."

"I had an incredibly long, wonderful marriage. I'm emerging into a new person. And I'm making it work," she adds.

One reason she's making it work is that she's doing things her way, refusing to listen to the suggestions of others. She's not selling her home, where she and her husband raised their children. "This house is so Fillmore," she insists. "So are my life and my children. I have happy memories here. I'd hate to leave."

Today, Fillmore's ashes sit in an urn by Beverly's bedstand. Although he requested having his remains scattered on Catalina Island, where he loved to sail, Beverly has not granted his wish. "I don't want to take him away from here," she says softly, "I want him here. I can't let him go."

## KITTY CARLISLE HART

*"My dear, it's madness. I never say no to anything. It's made such a good life for me!"*

In 1911, Kitty Carlisle Hart was born in New Orleans, Louisiana, the only child of a doctor. When she was ten her father died, and she moved to Europe with her mother, Hortense Conn, who hoped to make valuable connections with wealthy socialites.

Kitty married famous playwright and director Moss Hart, who introduced her to the magical world of the Broadway theater, in 1946. But throughout the marriage, Kitty cultivated her own interests and created her own magic as well. For 21 years, she starred on the quiz show *To Tell the Truth*. In 1961, at the unfortunate death of her husband, Kitty became a single mom, raising her two children, Cathy, 11, and Chris, 13, alone.

As a widow, Kitty, now 90, continued to live a rich, dynamic life. An admitted late bloomer, she returned to singing, debuting at the Metropolitan Opera at the age of 54. And at 64 she became chairman of the New York Arts Council, raising millions of dollars for performing artists, museums, schools, and arts-in-education programs throughout the state.

---

There is nothing like a dame. And Kitty Carlisle Hart is a great one. She, and other women of her time, are portrayed in Marie Brenner's hit book *Great Dames* as women who "had this rather amazing combination of courage and nobility displayed in cashmere and pearls. They were warriors in high heels."

And Kitty Carlisle Hart, 90, widow of the famous playwright and theatrical director Moss Hart, continues to be a warrior. She attributes this to her gutsy attitude. "Almost every morning I look in the mirror, saying, 'I forgive you for all the bad things you did the day before.' Then, I face a new day."

When her husband died, she'd been happily married for 15 years. She remembers that her grief lasted longer than expected. "It takes about two years to put things together," she explains. "At the beginning of the second year, you expect to feel better and then you don't. It's hard. It's very hard."

How does she suggest coping with the death of your husband? "Accept everything that comes along, and out of that will evolve something you really want to do," she says matter-of-factly. "That's how I got involved in the arts, and they've been my life."

Through her passions, she discovered a zest for living alone. From 1956 to 1977 she starred on the TV program *To Tell The Truth*, where she became known for her wit, verve, and intelligence. But she did more. In fact, nothing could stop her. "Everything was gratifying. I did everything late in life," she says. "I made my debut at the Metropolitan Opera at the age of 54 in a leading role, and I became chairman of the New York Arts Council when most people are retiring—at 64."

Mrs. Hart's ability to dazzle the rural legislators in Albany has most likely preserved the New York State Council on the Arts. In her book, Marie Brenner says that people describe Mrs. Hart as a person who "lights up a room," or "exudes radiance."

As chairman of the arts council, her tact was charming but tough. "You may think that your highway budget is important," she says, addressing a state legislator, "but nothing is more important than money for the arts—this is a matter of the soul."

And where does she get her energy? Kitty Carlisle Hart attributes it to sheer survival strength. Kitty was the only child of Hortense Conn, a determined woman given to mood swings. After her father died when she was ten, Kitty's mother sold their home and moved to Europe, grooming her daughter to marry into nobility. While staying at the least expensive rooms in the best hotels, her mother would ingratiate herself to European society, getting invitations from the elite. Kitty carried her mother's heavy baggage off trains, while her mother pretended to be a wealthy woman with servants behind her.

Kitty learned to fear these trips. By the age of 11 she felt like an outsider, pushing herself into places where she didn't belong. In her memoir *Kitty* she writes: "Before I went into a room, my mother would pinch me in the back and hiss, 'Be gracious!' And I always was."

And so began Kitty's training at combining charm with grit and determination. "When my mother got angry, it was monumental. But I learned when I was 14 that if I could amuse her, tell her an interesting story about something that had happened to me, I could turn her wrath away. That taught me early on that you get along much better and get what you want by being charming, not by being sullen or angry."

Though Kitty never married royalty, she did marry Moss Hart in 1946. He was a fresh, new playwright and director who at 26 was already well known as the "prince of Broadway." His famous plays were *You Can't Take it With You* and *The Man Who Came to Dinner*, which he wrote with George Kaufman. Later he directed such shows as *My Fair Lady* and *Camelot.*

Moss introduced Kitty to the world of the Broadway theater. She quit singing and became a glamorous hostess, entertaining at lavish parties they gave in their luxurious home on Park Avenue. But, like Kitty's mother, Moss Hart demanded her constant presence. Author of the popular autobiography *Act One,* he worked at home and they ate lunch together every day. "We lived in each other's pockets," says Mrs. Hart.

In the evenings, Moss and Kitty attended parties, where Moss would often dictate what Kitty would wear and with whom she'd speak. "I admired him very much," she confessed. "I thought he was a genius. I played a secondary role, but it wasn't my life. It was his life. I lived my mother's life until I got married. I did what she wanted me to do. Then, I lived my husband's life until he died.

"Then, I began to live my own life."

When Moss died in 1961, Kitty started over. With two children, ages 11 and 13, she moved from Palm Springs back to Manhattan. As she adjusted to being single, she discovered something about herself.

"I find living on my own extremely pleasant," she says, laughing. And her secret is keeping busy. A staunch defender of the arts, she became chairwoman of the New York State Council of the Arts, where she has remained for 21 years. In her role as leader of the Council, she travels the state checking on 1,300 groups, like the Frederic Chopin Singing Society of Buffalo, the Iroquois Indian Museum in Schoharie County, the New York Latvian

Concert Choir, and the Billie Holiday Theater in Bedford-Stuyvesant.

But that's not all. Her ability to shape a new life for herself has led her to other interests as well.

Mrs. Hart is now preparing for a concert in which she will be touring throughout the country. "Now, I have a whole new life," she exclaims. "Most women my age are sitting around twiddling their thumbs, going to the doctor. So, I've been very lucky."

As you travel the sometimes bumpy road to living on your own, you may be surprised at what you discover, including talents that have been hidden throughout your marriage.

Whether you're taking charge of your money, applying for a new job, joining a support group, or throwing a party for widowed or divorced friends (or both), this is your time.

As Liz Carpenter says, "Many women will live one-third of their lives alone, so it's important to show an interest in others, develop a sense of purpose and, most important of all, be good to yourself."

Living alone can teach you new skills. It can make you stronger. It can make you more independent. And with a new sense of freedom, you'll discover that living alone is not just a transitional phase, but provides a rich, full life of opportunities and adventure.

After reaping the rewards of living alone, you may choose to remain single, shaping your own destiny and relishing your solitude. As you realize your new potential, you'll learn to be at peace with living alone . . . and, as others have found, you may love it!

## AGING

American Association of Retired Persons
601 E. Street NW
Washington, D.C. 20049
Phone: (202) 434-2243
Fax: (202) 434-7680

Administration on Aging
3330 Independence Avenue SW
Washington, D.C. 20201
Phone: (202) 619-0724

Eldercare Support Services
3330 Independence Avenue NW
Washington, D.C. 20201
Phone: (800) 766-1116

iVillage
www.iVillage.com

National Center on Women and Aging
Phyllis Mutschler, Executive Director
Brandeis University
Waltham, MA 02254-9110
Phone: (781) 736-3863

National Center on Women and Retirement Research
South Hampton College
Long Island University
South Hampton, New York 11968
Phone: (800) 426-7386

National Council on Aging
409 3rd St. SW, Suite 200
Washington, D.C. 20024
Phone: (202) 479-1200
www.ncoa.org

Supportive Older Women's Network (SOWN)
2805 N. 47th St.
Philadelphia, PA 19131
Phone: (215) 477-6000

## DIVORCE

Fisher Seminars
Jere Bierhaus, Director
7845 Gunnison Place
Denver, CO 80231
Phone: (303) 696-8101

DivorceSupport.com
www.divorcesupport.com

Divorce Source
www.divorcesource.com

Information and Resources for Suddenly Single Parents
www.divorceandchildren.com

## CHILD CARE

IRS
Child Care Credit
Child and Dependent Care Publication 503
Phone: (800) TAXFORM
www.irs.gov

*Unofficial Guide to Childcare,* by Ann Douglas.
*Tips on childcare opportunities, focusing on cost and quality.*
www.childcare-guide.com/cost.htm

## GRIEF

AARP Grief and Loss Program
*(formerly Widowed Persons Service)*
601 East St. NW
Washington, D.C. 20049
Phone: (202) 434-2260
www.aarp.org/griefandloss

Association for Death Education and Counseling (ADEC)
638 Prospect Ave.
Hartford, CT 06105-4298
Phone: (202) 232-4825
Fax: (203) 232-0819
www.adec.org

The Centering Group
*A non-profit organization providing supportive grief literature and work-shops for families.*
1531 Saddle Creek Road
Omaha, NE 68104-5064
Phone: (402) 553-1200

International THEOS Foundation
322 Boulevard of the Allies, Suite 105
Pittsburgh, PA 15222-1919
Phone: (412) 471-7779
Fax: (412) 471-7782

Older Women's League (OWL)
666 11th St. NW, Suite 700
Washington, D.C. 20001
Phone: (202) 783-6686

Shiva Foundation
551 Cordova Rd., #709
Santa Fe, NM 87501
Phone: (800) 720-9544
www.goodgrief.org
E-mail: shiva@goodgrief.org

WidowNet
www.fortnet.org/widownet

## HEALTH

American Psychiatric Association
1400 K Street NW
Washington, D.C. 20005
Phone: (202) 682-6000

National Institute of Mental Health
*Provides free brochures on depression and its treatment.*
60001 Executive Blvd.
Room 8181, MSC9663
Bethesda, MD 20892
Phone: (800) 421-4211

National Mental Health Association
1021 Prince Street
Alexandria, VA 22314-2971
Phone: (800) 969-NMHA
www.nmha.org

National Women's Health Information Center
*Provides literature and information pertaining to women's health issues.*
8550 Arlington Blvd., Suite 300
Fairfax, VA 22031
Phone: (703) 560-6619
(800) 944-WOMAN
www.4woman.gov

## MOVING

Allied Van Lines
www.alliedvan.com

Atlas Van Lines
www.atlasvanlines.com

The Relocation Experts
*Offers moving cost estimates, tips, real estate listings,*
*insurance and storage.*
www.moving.com

## SELF-ESTEEM

American Association of University Women
*Provides ongoing studies pertaining to self-esteem.*
1111 Sixteenth Street NW
Washington, D.C. 20036
Phone: (800) 326-AAUW
www.aauw.org

Women of Wisdom (WOW)
Susie Smoot-Brown, Director
Brookhaven Community College
3939 Valley View Lane
Farmers Branch, Texas 75244-4997
Phone: (972) 860-4153

## SINGLE PARENTING

About.com: The Human Internet
*Single parenting.*
www.singleparenting.about.com/parenting/singleparenting

Parents Without Partners International, Inc.
1650 South Dixie Hwy., Suite 510
Boca Raton, FL 33432
Phone: (561) 391-8833
www.parentswithoutpartners.org

Single Parents Association
Phone: (800) 704-2102
(602) 788-5511 (in Arizona)
E-mail: Info@singleparents.org

Single Parents World
www.parentsworld.com

Society for the Prevention of Cruelty to Children (SPCC)
161 Williams Street, 12th Floor
New York, New York 10038
Phone: (800) 447-7220

Supervised Visitation Network
*This service is used for parents in child custody disputes who have difficulty confronting each other.*
Phone: (800) 447-7220

## FINANCING, WILLS, AND ESTATE PLANNING

National Association of Financial and Estate Planning
525 E. 4500 South, #F-100
Salt Lake City, UT 84107
Phone: (801) 266-9900
Fax: (801) 266-1019
E-mail: nafep@nafep.com

Nolo.com—Law for All
www.nolo.com

# Bibliography

Besson, Taunee S. *National Business Employment Weekly Resumes.*
New York: John Wiley and Sons, 1994.

Bolles, Richard Nelson. *What Color Is Your Parachute?* Berkeley,
CA: Ten Speed Press,1995.

Brenner, Marie. *Great Dames.* New York: Crown, 2000.

Carpenter, Liz. *Getting Better All the Time.* New York: Simon &
Schuster, 1987.

———. *Unplanned Parenthood: Confessions of a Septuagenarian Surrogate Mother.* New York: Random House, 1994.

———. "Panache After 50." *New Choices,* May 1997, p.52.

Davidson, Jeff. *The Complete Idiot's Guide to Assertiveness.* Indianapo-
lis, IN: Macmillan, 1997.

Davis, Verdell. *Let Me Grieve, But Not Forever.* Nashville, TN: Word
Publishing, 1997.

Douglas, Ann. *The Unofficial Guide to Childcare.* Foster City, CA:
IDG Books, 1998.

Downey, Sarah. "The Moving Van Wars." *Newsweek,* February 27,
2000.

Dychtwald, Ken. *Age Wave.* New York: Bantam. 1990.

Elkind, David. *The Hurried Child.* Reading, MA: Addison Wesley,
1981.

Fisher, Bruce. *Rebuilding: When Your Relationship Ends.* San Luis
Obispo, CA: Impact Publishers, 1992.

Fitzgerald, Helen. *The Grieving Child.* Upper Saddle River, NJ:
Simon & Schuster, 1992.

Gray, John. *Men Are from Mars, Women Are from Venus.* New York:
HarperCollins, 1992.

Hannon, Kerry. *Ten Minute Guide to Retirement for Women.* Old Tappan, NJ: Macmillan, 1997.

———. *Suddenly Single: Money Skills for Divorcees and Widows.* New York: John Wiley and Sons, 1998.

Jowell, Barbara Tom, and Donnette Schwisow. *After He's Gone: A Guide for Widowed and Divorced Women.* Secaucus, NJ: Birch Lane Press/Carol Publishing Group, 1997.

Little, Mary Ann. *Loving Your Children Better: Matching Parenting Strategies to the Age and Stage of Your Children.* Kansas City, MO: Westport Publishers, 1991.

Orman, Suze. *The 9 Steps to Financial Freedom.* New York: Crown Publishers, 1997.

———. *The Courage to Be Rich.* New York: Putnam, 1999.

Quinn, Jane Bryant. *Making the Most of Your Money.* New York: Simon & Schuster, 1991.

Rivers, Joan. *Bouncing Back.* New York: HarperCollins, 1997.

———. *From Mother to Daughter: Thoughts and Advice on Life, Love and Marriage.* Secaucus, NJ: Birch Lane Press, 1998.

———. Interview by Gia Kourlas. "The Hot Seat—Small Talk with Big People. Cry Me a River." *Time Out New York,* 2000.

Savageau, David, and Ralph D'Agostino. *Places Rated Almanac.* New York: Macmillan General Reference, 1999.

Shropshire, Mike, and Frank Schaefer. *The Thorny Road to Texas.* New York: Birch Lane Press/Carol Publishing Group, 1994.

Snyderman, Nancy. *Guide to Good Health: What Every Forty-Plus Woman Should Know About Her Changing Body.* New York: William Morrow & Co., 1996.

———. *Necessary Journeys.* New York: Hyperion, 2000.

Wallenstein, Judith, and Sandra Blakeslee. *Second Chances.* New York: Ticknor & Fields, 1992.

Wetzstein, Cheryl. "Latchkey Children: Statistics Unlocked." *Washington Times,* April 13, 2000.

# Index

Pamela Stone will be available for speaking engagements, lectures, and seminars. She can be reached at Pamstone3@aol.com.

Made in the USA
Monee, IL
14 September 2022

13943137R00152